C000215276

MARTIN SCORSESE
IN TEN SCENES

MARTIN SCORSESE
IN TEN SCENES

TIM GRIERSON

CONTENTS

MARTIN SCORSESE IN TEN SCENES

An Hachette UK Company
www.hachette.co.uk

First published in the Unitred Kingdom in 2015 by
ILEX, a division of Octopus Publishing Group Ltd

Octopus Publishing Group
Carmelite House
50 Victoria Embankment
London, EC4Y 0DZ
www.octopusbooks.co.uk

Design, layout, and text copyright
© Octopus Publishing Group 2015

Publisher: Roly Allen
Commissioning Editor: Zara Larcombe
Editor: Rachel Silverlight
Senior Project Editor: Natalia Price-Cabrera
Managing Specialist Editor: Frank Gallaugher
Art Director: Julie Weir
Designers: Grade Design
Picture Research: Claire Gouldstone
Senior Production Controller: Sarah Kramer

All rights reserved. No part of this work may
be reproduced or utilized in any form or by
any means, electronic or mechanical, including
photocopying, recording or by any information
storage and retrieval system, without the prior
written permission of the publisher.

Tim Grierson asserts the moral right to be
identified as the author of this work.

ISBN 978-1-78157-306-8

A CIP catalogue record for this book is available
from the British Library

Printed and bound in China

10 9 8 7 6 5 4 3 2 1

An early example of Scorsese using music to
provide energy and define character in his films.
Also, the innovative camerawork, which required
strapping the camera onto Harvey Keitel's shoulders,
suggested a liberating new way to think about
filmmaking during the early period of Hollywood's
renaissance of the 1970s.

This 1976 classic is sometimes misunderstood to
be an apology for (or a promotion of) sociopathic
violence, but this bravura sequence strongly refutes
such claims. Despite its technical skill, the sequence
doesn't celebrate violence but, rather, shows the sheer
futility of such behavior.

Scorsese's sensitivity to the warmth and power
of rock 'n' roll was never better captured than in
this documentary concert film of The Band's final
performance. This song in particular demonstrates
his ability to show the bittersweet emotions, the
intimacy and tension, of veteran musicians in
the midst of their grand farewell.

6  **7**  **8**  **9**  **10**

FOREWORD

IN THE FALL OF 1973 I was invited to see *Mean Streets* at the New York Film Festival. Afterwards, I met this bearded, dynamic young man—Marty Scorsese—and remarked to him that not only did I admire *Mean Streets* a great deal, but I also wanted to know how he came to place the poster of one of my first films, *Point Blank*, in this film. The poster image of Lee Marvin with a gun was positioned so that it was pointing right at Bob De Niro's head, just before he gets murdered in *Mean Streets*. It turned out we had the same taste in movies. *Point Blank* was an innovative film for the late '60s and I think Marty was always kind of attracted to that format. So it was part homage, but it also worked well in *Mean Streets* because it foreshadowed what was about to become of Bob's character.

We've had a close relationship ever since. Marty and I share similar backgrounds, growing up in New York City. Marty was brought up on the Lower East Side of Manhattan in an Italian-American family. My father worked in that area and we were Jewish Americans. Our connection grew closer when Marty called me about a script he'd heard I had that dealt with the big-band era: *New York, New York*. Although, like a great many films, the idea of the script was more attractive than the script itself. We bravely decided to do it together and that started a working relationship that continues now over 40 years later, with my producing Marty's current film, *Silence*.

Marty takes risks, that's why I love him and that's why actors love him. The actors want to work with him because their performances show the risks that Marty encourages them to take.

On *New York, New York*, I got a first-hand lesson in authenticity and emotion from Marty. We were shooting the marriage proposal scene with Bob De Niro and Liza Minnelli on a set that Boris Leven had designed. The scene had Bob and Liza driving up to a Justice of the Peace, getting out of the car and walking up to a glass-paned door. When Bob did the first take he knocked on the glass and it broke. Marty wanted to take advantage of that very realistic moment, the kind you couldn't make up—a couple trying to get married and, of all things, glass breaks when they knock at the Justice of the Peace's door. Marty said, "That's real, let's do it that way." We then had to send out the prop man to buy glass that would shatter safely and properly. Marty rehearsed the actors during that period and when the prop man returned, he replaced the glass in the door. Every time we did another take, the shattered glass had to be cleaned up and the prop glass had to be reinserted—and all of this took quite a bit of time.

As we kept going, and it was getting later and later, I was concerned that the overtime would impact the following day's shoot. We were scheduled to shoot an exterior scene and if we didn't finish promptly we would be in a forced turnaround situation and wouldn't be able to get the actors and crew until well into the day, which meant that we would have a very short shooting period that day. When I discussed it with Marty, he said to me, "In the last take, I really think I saw a tear in the corner of Liza's eye. Do you want me to stop or do you want me to go for the tear?" Well, I've always tried for the tear and the emotion ever since.

I've had the good fortune to be able to watch Marty extract authentic emotion from his actors for many years, such as the violent emotion of the characters that Bob De Niro and Joe Pesci played out with Cathy Moriarty in *Raging Bull*. To me, one of the singular scenes of love, animosity, and violence is Jake LaMotta chasing and catching his wife, and then pummeling his brother in a rage of jealousy. I've witnessed a character go from comedy and friendship to sudden expressions of violence and fear in the "You think I'm funny" scene with Joe Pesci and Ray Liotta in *Goodfellas*. And in *The Wolf of Wall Street*, you have the attempted lovemaking between Leo DiCaprio and Margot Robbie that goes from their bed to the nursery and to the spousal animosity that plunges to a very dark place in these characters' lives.

Marty is the most open artist I've ever worked with. He encourages collaboration and opinions, and the actors and technicians always seem to want to please.

ABOVE: Martin Scorsese and Irwin Winkler on the set of 2016's *Silence*.

And, of course, Marty loves actors. He has a great rapport with his actors and they love him because of his passion.

Just recently, on the set of *Silence* in Taipei, I saw Adam Driver (forty pounds thinner than when he started the movie) jump into icy cold water many times and swim out to sea—no stunt double—to try to save a drowning woman. Only for Marty Scorsese are we all willing to jump into the cold and deep.

I hope that you too will discover the many sides of Marty's genius in this book, scene by scene.

Irwin Winkler
June, 2015

INTRODUCTION

SOME FILMMAKERS' WORK is so distinctive visually and thematically that you could identify their aesthetic fingerprints simply by watching a few moments from any of their movies. An oeuvre can demonstrate the breadth of that artist's personal obsessions and narrative interests, but sometimes a single scene—or a collection of scenes—can reveal the building blocks for that filmmaker's creative DNA.

One such director is Martin Scorsese, who is among the most acclaimed living American filmmakers, his professional career spanning almost 50 years. But setting aside for a minute the Academy Awards won by actors and craftspeople working on his films, his Best Director Oscar for *The Departed*, and his box office successes, Scorsese should be celebrated primarily for being a hugely influential artist whose vibrant work has proved an inspiration for a whole host of directors, most notably Quentin Tarantino, Spike Lee, and Paul Thomas Anderson. But what are the foundations of his genius? What moments define his singular talent?

Martin Scorsese in Ten Scenes tries to answer those questions. As the title suggests, *Ten Scenes* attempts to encapsulate Scorsese's mastery through ten indelible sequences from his movies, examining not just what makes these scenes so terrific but, more crucially, why only this specific director could have brought them to such vivid life.

Selecting these scenes proved to be a challenge—a fun one, but also daunting. At the time of writing, Scorsese has directed 23 features—his 24th, *Silence*, due in 2016—and has made numerous documentaries, shorts, and music videos. With Scorsese, it's not a question of having enough memorable scenes but, instead, trying to narrow down from an imposing

list of highlight moments. So while he has several classics to his name—*Raging Bull, Goodfellas, Taxi Driver*—I didn't want to focus entirely on obvious choices. To be sure, those three movies are all included, but scenes from, say, *The Last Waltz* (his powerfully emotional concert documentary about The Band) and *Gangs of New York* (his long-delayed and problematic nineteenth-century epic) are, to my mind, just as important in assessing what has made him such a relentlessly ambitious and passionate filmmaker.

No doubt some readers will disagree with my choices, which I hope will spark reflection on Scorsese's lasting legacy. After so many years, it's clear that he is not a director who produces only one kind of movie: He has given us crime thrillers (*The Departed*), family films (*Hugo*), heartbreaking psychological horror movies (*Shutter Island*), dark comedies (*After Hours*), biopics (*The Aviator*), religious dramas (*The Last Temptation of Christ, Kundun*), compelling character studies (*Raging Bull, Taxi Driver, The King of Comedy*) and a few films that speak to his Little Italy childhood (*Mean Streets, Goodfellas*). No one book could hope to be a definitive summation of such a multifaceted talent, so let *Ten Scenes* get the conversation started, rather than serving as the final word.

Each chapter is built around an individual scene. Punctuated by existing interviews with actors, cinematographers, production designers, and others who collaborated with Scorsese—as well as insights from the director himself—*Ten Scenes* seeks to understand the artistic and personal impulses that went into such groundbreaking moments. For example, the boxing sequences in *Raging Bull* are justifiably admired for their savagery and craftsmanship, but understanding that Scorsese was never a sports fan adds an extra dimension of appreciation for what he achieved—as well as the fact that he initially resisted Robert De Niro's overtures to make the movie. (*Raging Bull*, by the way, wasn't the only time Scorsese needed encouragement from those close to him to pursue a project that would help define his career.) Considering that he's one of the most studied and vaunted filmmakers of our era, it can be difficult to appraise Scorsese's oeuvre with fresh eyes. By looking at individual moments rather than a complete body of work, *Ten Scenes* invites readers to reenter the world of a master.

I approached this book with an eye toward inspiring aspiring filmmakers, which explains why each chapter ends with a breakdown of specific techniques and aesthetics used in the particular scene. But I found the exercise also helpful for me as a critic and writer—forcing me to pin down, for instance, exactly why my chosen scene from *The King of Comedy* has haunted me ever since I first saw it decades ago. But what I hope comes across is that Scorsese's brilliance can't be reduced to a bullet-point list of to-do items. Any of us could physically reproduce these scenes with the use of cameras, lights, and actors—but there is something ineffable, out of reach, that keeps us from fully emulating what Scorsese has achieved, and continues to achieve, in his films. No book could pin down his genius, so let us join together in celebrating a collection of scenes that captivate every time we watch them.

There are several people to thank for the beautiful book you now hold in your hands. The first is Zara Larcombe, who has shepherded this project from the start. Then, we must acknowledge the tireless efforts of Nick Jones, Frank Gallaugher, and most especially Rachel Silverlight, who was the kind steward from across the pond during this book's production. And I have to thank the entire staff of Ilex and Octopus. My association with these good people began in 2010, when my *Screen International* editor Mike Goodridge invited me to collaborate with him on *FilmCraft: Cinematography*, which opened the door to me editing the screenwriting edition a few years later. I'm immensely proud of the books I've made with Ilex/Octopus, and much of the credit goes to the company's exceptional team. Like a film, these books are a team effort, and I'm grateful to everyone who pitched in.

Lastly, I want to thank my parents, Bob and Debbie, who couldn't have imagined where my life would have led when they sent me off to film school so long ago. My sister Lisa will hopefully get around to watching *There Will Be Blood* and *The Social Network* one of these days. And then there's my wife Susan, who I think loves *Shutter Island* as much as I do—or at least loves what I love so much about it. Thank you for the endless smiles, honey.

Tim Grierson
Los Angeles, California
January 2015

MEAN STREETS

1973

SCREENPLAY:
Martin Scorsese and Mardik Martin

CINEMATOGRAPHER:
Kent Wakeford

EDITOR:
Sid Levin

PRINCIPAL SCENE ACTOR:
Harvey Keitel (Charlie Cappa)

SCENE:
The drunk tracking shot

I. INTRODUCTION

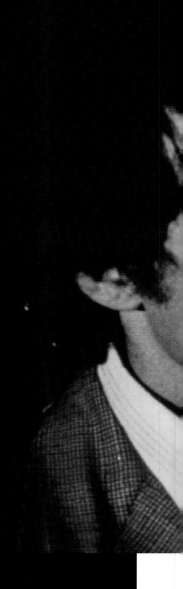

Martin Scorsese's first unqualified success, *Mean Streets* ripples with themes that would become hallmarks for the rest of his career. Catholic guilt, the toxicity of masculinity, the allure of the criminal lifestyle, the dangerous energy of New York City, the marriage of indelible image and iconic pop music—all these things have a place in this tale of a low-level hood hoping to work his way up the ladder of the East Coast Mafia.

Harvey Keitel plays Charlie Cappa, whose friendship with Johnny Boy Civello (Robert De Niro, working with Scorsese for the first time) may prove to be his undoing. (Unlike the even-tempered Charlie, Johnny Boy is a hothead ready to explode at any moment.) But *Mean Streets*' most resonant scene involves just Keitel and contains no dialogue, a beautiful example at an early age of Scorsese's skill at making emotional, evocative cinema that's both simple and innovative.

In the span of about 80 seconds, we see Charlie as he enjoys a night out drinking. He seems to be floating around the room: euphoric, intoxicated, sweating, flirting, and finally passing out. It's an extraordinary way to capture the rush of being young and feeling indestructible, and the scene showcases Scorsese's ability to find the perfect visual (and musical) expression of a character's inner self.

ABOVE: Harvey Keitel and Robert De Niro in *Mean Streets*. The characters they play in this film—Charlie Cappa and Johnny Boy, respectively—are not the hardened mobsters of *Goodfellas*, but ordinary young men from the streets of Little Italy.

II.KEITEL

Before Robert De Niro became Scorsese's most recognizable onscreen proxy, there was Harvey Keitel, who starred in Scorsese's debut, *Who's That Knocking at My Door*. A more reserved actor than De Niro, Keitel brought a pathos to Charlie, but also a fresh-faced yearning beneath the character's tough exterior. Even in this wordless scene in *Mean Streets*, which Charlie floats through in a drunken haze, there's an openness to the performance; Keitel delivers the sense of a young man whose whole life stretches out in front of him—as long as he makes the right decisions.

"Most of my directions are really less: 'Less, please, less,'" Scorsese said about working with actors in a 1975 interview. "Or when I want a guy to get mad, like Harvey Keitel, smashing through the window, I didn't have to tell him anything. Nothing. Harvey did that. He knows. He was feeling that. I didn't have to tell him anything."

"I didn't think I was particularly good at [acting] but I wanted to be, I had a strong will to be good at it," Keitel said in 1992, reflecting on the early days of his career. "And it was my need to know, my need to draw my pictures on the cave walls about what my fears were, what my needs were. Somewhere in there. I was in a cave and I needed to draw some pictures on the wall about what my journey was, and that drive, that need, led me to acting. I wasn't good at it, but I had a deep, intense desire to be good at it, and all my failings didn't stop me. I had that will to learn

BELOW: Harvey Keitel in *Mean Streets*.

that kept me going through all my effort, through all of my struggle."

Keitel came up at the same time as Scorsese, and he recalled what it was like to work with the young director.

"I sort of taught him in a way everything he knows, because one day on the set of *Mean Streets* I taught him a very important lesson which I'm sure made his whole career," the actor recollected. "He was talking to me about a scene, he was saying, 'Well, Harvey, this thing and that thing,' it was getting very sort of deeply psychological and [he was] trying to find the right words to help me understand the scene and to go in a certain direction. He's trying to be gentle and motivative and he was going on and on and on, and I said, 'Marty, you mean be better?' He said, 'Yeah!'"

ABOVE: Harvey Keitel and Martin Scorsese on the set of *Taxi Driver*.

ABOVE: Harvey Keitel with Zina Bethune in Scorsese's debut film, *Who's That Knocking at My Door*.

ABOVE: Harvey Keitel's Charlie Cappa floats through the scene in a drunken stupor, until finally passing out.

III. THE SETUP

In the scene, Charlie appears to be stationary, while the background moves behind him. To achieve the effect, Scorsese and cinematographer Kent Wakeford attached a camera to the front of Harvey Keitel that faced the actor.

This device would come to be known as the SnorriCam, named after Eidur Snorri and Einar Snorri, the (unrelated) Icelandic filmmakers who pioneered its use. As they describe on their website, the SnorriCam technique allows for "a visceral and dynamic camera angle that stabilizes the person it's pointing at no matter how they move. It is often used to isolate and focus on an introspective, dangerous or exhilarating moment in a film. It requires no operation of the camera, once the rig is set the actor controls the camera with his/her movements."

The SnorriCam was patented in the mid-1990s, but Scorsese's use of a mounted camera in *Mean Streets* helped popularize this expressive camera style decades earlier. As Charlie floats through the room, the audience gets the sensation of being drunk: we lose our balance and everything feels heightened, almost dreamlike. *Mean Streets* is a film that emphasizes realism, which makes brief, stylized interludes like this scene all the more affecting. Just as the Snorris describe, the use of the technique in this scene takes you inside Charlie's world.

"The Aeroflex camera was relatively light so I hooked the shoulder unit I created to Harvey Keitel and turned the camera using a wide-angle lens around to face him," cinematographer Kent Wakeford explained in 2009. "Harvey stumbled through the bar, with the batteries tied around his waist. Martin and I were right there with him, ducking out of light and shadows. Originally, the scene was set to end as he fell. But, as Harvey hit the floor, he stayed in character and passed out. When we saw the footage, we loved it."

HOMEMADE FEEL

Scorsese and *Mean Streets* cinematographer Kent Wakeford have both been justly praised for the film's original look and feel. Partly, the unique look came down to a limited budget—Scorsese had tried to interest Roger Corman, who had produced Scorsese's previous film, *Boxcar Bertha*, in financing *Mean Streets*, but Corman would only agree to do it if Scorsese made the characters black. Even after finding a backer in Jonathan Taplin, road manager for The Band at the time, they simply didn't have the money for a big production, so they had to get creative and work with what they had. (For example, only six days of shooting for this quintessential New-York-City film actually took place in New York—using a student crew and without permits. Most of the film was shot in L.A., reminding us that so much of filmmaking is about illusion.)

But key is the innovative lighting and camerawork. The state-of-the-art SnorriCam technique was used to such great effect in this scene, but Wakeford's handheld camera techniques and use of shadowy lighting throughout the film so perfectly capture the grittiness of the streets and the messy lives of those who live in them.

BELOW: Kent Wakeford, cinematographer for *Mean Streets* and *Alice Doesn't Live Here Anymore*, standing behind Scorsese on the set of *Mean Streets*.

ABOVE: Harvey Keitel and Cesare Danova in *Mean Streets*. An eclectic, often surprising, and frequently inspired use of music has come to be a key feature of Scorsese's films.

IV. THE SONG

Scorsese receives sufficient credit for helping introduce the concept of using popular music as a way to score a film. But what's overlooked in a movie like *Mean Streets*, where he first used this technique, was that it wasn't simply pop and rock music on the soundtrack—opera and doo-wop are also prominent. For the director, the many different styles featured weren't so incongruous:

"It was literally the way you hear it [growing up]," Scorsese said in 2011, "particularly if there was a street [festival] going on… [You'd hear the band playing] the Italian national anthem … all these Neapolitan songs, some Sicilian songs, and they became part of

your subconscious, because twice or three times a year that was happening outside the window since you were a child… That became part of the scoring of your life."

Scorsese recalled that his neighborhood served as an international jukebox when he was a boy. "All this [different music] would weave in and out of the windows," he once said. "Especially in the summer, the windows were open, the doors were open, there was no air-conditioning, no fans. Everybody was living in an interesting kind of dorm, in a way. People sleeping on fire escapes … it all sounds very, very romantic, but actually it was pretty miserable."

ABOVE: Martin Scorsese with Keitel and De Niro on the set of *Mean Streets*.

RIGHT: The Chips.

The song used to score this scene was The Chips' "Rubber Biscuit," and its goofy spirit and nonsensical lyrics both complement and contradict what's happening on the screen. The 1956 doo-wop tune is catchy but strange: The vocals are a combination of scat and spoken-word, and the jaunty melody is several degrees brighter than *Mean Streets*' dark tenor. But it gives an energy to the scene that's as startling in its own way as the use of the unusual camera setup. In one sense, "Rubber Biscuit" is just another way for Scorsese to disorient us, and yet the song's giddy ridiculousness also articulates the euphoria and fogginess of staggering around drunk in public.

ABOVE: Stills from Cassavetes' experimental 1959 feature, *Shadows*.

BELOW: John Cassavetes at work.

V. THE SHADOW OF CASSAVETES

A voracious film lover, Scorsese drew on many inspirations to make the freewheeling *Mean Streets*. But one of the primary influences was John Cassavetes, a New York writer-director who helped pioneer the low-budget American independent movement of the 1960s, especially with his 1959 feature, *Shadows*, an improvisational portrait of the city's young people, which counted no stars and was shot with lightweight cameras.

"Cassavetes was the one to really push us over the edge... He did it so openly and honestly," Scorsese recalled in 2011. "The style was in the making of the film, in a way, the passion of making the film. You say, 'Well, it was grainy and looked documentary': It doesn't matter, it doesn't matter. 'Oh, he paid no attention to production design': I'm sure he did, you see? But it's another way of looking at it."

Watching a Cassavetes film, Scorsese said, made him feel like, "We could do anything... We could get away with the style, because we had to reinvent the style at that time. Cassavetes was the one who really pushed us to do that. ...People [at the time] always talked about, 'I'm going to make a film, I'm going to make a film, but I don't have enough money.' When I saw *Shadows*, I said, 'There's no more excuses.'"

Cassavetes's influence was felt on *Mean Streets* in another way, too. Speaking with film critic Richard

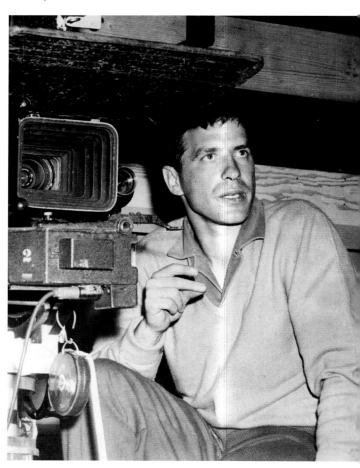

SCORSESE & THE MOB

Mean Streets is the film that marks the beginning of Scorsese's interest in mobsters, a fascination that would continue through films such as *Goodfellas*, *Casino*, and *The Departed*. Interestingly, *Mean Streets* opened on the heels of *The Godfather*, which was a commercial and critical success, winning the Oscar for Best Picture. The close proximity between the two films' releases was purely coincidental, though.

"Mardik Martin and I wrote the screenplay for *Mean Streets* seven years ago, so we could hardly have been influenced by *The Godfather*," Scorsese explained in 1973. "We weren't trying to do the same sort of thing at all. Francis Coppola made an epic Hollywood picture, an old-fashioned movie—in the good sense—like *Gone with the Wind*, only better."

In contrast to Coppola's epic, which revolves around the rich and powerful Corleone family, Scorsese's film focuses on the young up-and-comers trying to establish themselves in the mob, the guys he knew growing up. "[T]he majority of the people in Little Italy are decent, hardworking people," he said. "But there is also this milieu of young turks. Some people are shocked that these guys are running around, buying and selling hot stuff. But *I'm* not shocked—I'll buy toothpaste from them for 19 cents instead of 50 cents. Why not? It's not as if they're dealing in heroin. And don't forget, even numbers runners are hardworking guys."

What comes through is that *Mean Streets* is a film about a world Scorsese knows from his own experience, and it's an accurate portrayal of the people who occupy it, and so it found fans both in high-minded critics and the people it was about alike. "I'll get into a cab sometimes here in New York, and they'll know who I am and the film they'll bring up is *Mean Streets*... 'Aaah, you'll never beat that, kid, that was the best one...' That sorta stuff."

ABOVE: *The Godfather* remains one of the most influential films of the 1970s.

Schickel, Scorsese noted that Cassavetes had urged him to make *Mean Streets* because he had disliked *Boxcar Bertha*, Scorsese's previous film. Recalled Scorsese, "He said, 'You just spent a year of your life making a piece of shit.' He said, 'The actors are good. I can tell you like the actors. It's a lot of fun. But you shouldn't do that kind of picture. After *Who's That Knocking*, you've got to do something you really feel.'"

Cassavetes, who was never afraid to make a film the audience didn't like or didn't get, urged Scorsese not to get into the "exploitation business" but to make the films he really wanted to do. So Scorsese told Cassavetes about *Mean Streets*—then titled *Season of the Witch*—which needed rewriting. Cassavetes told the young director, "Do it."

VI. THE IMPACT

Just as Scorsese was inspired by the work of John Cassavetes, so too has *Mean Streets* proven a touchstone for future filmmakers. Its gritty, unglamorous portrait of down-and-dirty mob life helped influence (among others) *The Sopranos*, and the HBO show's star, James Gandolfini, cited it as one of his favorite movies.

But this individual scene looms just as large. The mounted-camera approach has been imitated in the work of Scorsese disciples such as Darren Aronofsky, who used it prominently in his early features *Pi* and *Requiem for a Dream*. But the filmmaker most associated with the technique has to be Spike Lee, whose variation on the visual strategy places both the camera and the actor on dollies. The director first incorporated it for *Mo' Better Blues*, describing the impetus as "show-offy, student film stuff." In a 2008 interview, Lee elaborated on his reasoning, saying, "You can get a transportive, or sometimes alienated feeling, depending on the situation of the scene."

RIGHT & OPPOSITE CENTER: Darren Aronofsky's early films are known for their prodigious use of the mounted-camera technique. At top, Sean Gullette in *Pi*, and below, Jennifer Connelly in *Requiem for a Dream*.

BELOW & OPPOSITE BOTTOM: Directors Darren Aronofsky (left) and Spike Lee (right).

SUMMARY OF TECHNIQUE

1. EXPRESSING THE INTERNAL VISUALLY

The SnorriCam technique allows a filmmaker to articulate character emotions in an unconventional way. Because of its jarring, imbalanced look, such shots seem to be reflecting the character's disheveled mindset. Scorsese used the technique to dramatize Charlie's drunken stupor, but other filmmakers have created feelings of alienation, addiction, paranoia, or menace with the SnorriCam.

2. GOING LIGHT

Liberated by the example of low-budget, experimental filmmakers like John Cassavetes, Scorsese and his cinematographer Kent Wakeford used light, cheap cameras to film *Mean Streets*. "Actors didn't have to hit their marks perfectly," Wakeford once said about using handheld cameras for much of the shoot. "They were able to be absorbed in the frenetic energy of their characters."

3. MUSIC

Mean Streets features a strikingly diverse collection of songs—everything from opera to rock 'n' roll—and Scorsese uses them to express the atmosphere he knew growing up in New York City. "I had no choice," he once said. "I didn't see it and I didn't hear it any other way." In this scene, the song choice adds another way of expressing the particular quality of the moment Keitel's Charlie is living through.

4. KNOWING A WORLD

Although Scorsese was never a mobster himself, he grew up around that world in Little Italy, absorbing its mores and culture. Those observed experiences inform the tone and feel of *Mean Streets*, adding authenticity to this specific coming-of-age story.

TAXI DRIVER
1976

SCREENPLAY:
Paul Schrader

CINEMATOGRAPHER:
Michael Chapman

EDITORS:
Tom Rolf
Melvin Shapiro

PRODUCTION DESIGNER:
Charles Rosen

PRINCIPAL SCENE ACTORS:
Robert De Niro (Travis Bickle)
Jodie Foster (Iris)
Harvey Keitel (Sport)

SCENE:
The hotel shoot-out

02

I. INTRODUCTION

Violence visits the characters in several Martin Scorsese pictures, but the filmmaker's relationship with violence was never more complicated than in *Taxi Driver*. A harrowing portrait of a Vietnam vet named Travis Bickle (Robert De Niro) living on the margins of New York City, *Taxi Driver* digs down into its protagonist's impotent rage: at the prostitutes and pimps he sees as he drives his cab every night; at the pretty political aide (Cybill Shepherd) who won't give him the time of day; at the ugliness and sin he wants to eradicate around him. It's a movie with a slow fuse, but one that we know will eventually go off.

And, at last, it does, in a brutal, blunt sequence near the end of the film as Travis attempts to rescue an underage hooker (Iris, played by Jodie Foster) from a slimy pimp (the colorfully named Sport, played by Scorsese's *Mean Streets* star Harvey Keitel). Travis considers himself to be a noble knight in shining armor, but his process of saving this young damsel in distress is through bloodshed, shooting his way into a cheap hotel and not stopping until everyone, save for Iris, is dead.

Sometimes misunderstood to be an apology for (or a promotion of) sociopathic violence, *Taxi Driver* finds a kind of catharsis in this bravura shootout, but the sequence strongly resists any notion of violence as liberation. Despite its technical skill, the sequence catalogs the sad horror and sheer pointlessness of macho swagger. This is catharsis without release, death with its sting intact.

LEFT: Robert De Niro and Martin Scorsese.

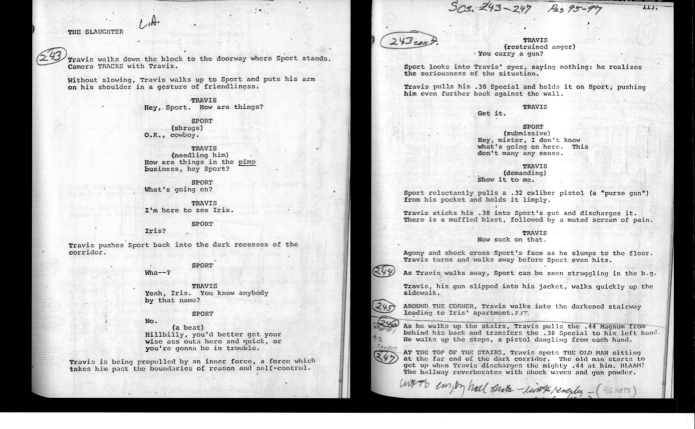

Scs. 243-247   Pgs 95-97   113.

II. THE SCREENPLAY

Taxi Driver has much to recommend it, and the whole cast and crew can take credit for the film's success. But the film's cinematographer, Michael Chapman, was clear on to whom the bulk of the praise belongs. "*Taxi Driver* is ultimately Paul Schrader's movie," he said in 1998. "His script remains the best I have ever read—not only in terms of its wrenching emotional content, but also because the pages dripped visual imagery. Marty did an incredible job with it (he has an instinctive understanding of the emotional content of a camera setup, like nobody else); Bobby De Niro was fantastic; but it's quite depressing to think that the greatest thing I've ever done was 25 years ago—and, unless I'm very lucky, I'll probably never get to do anything that powerful again."

Scorsese wouldn't disagree with Chapman's assertion about the film's true author. "I like Bob in it. Oh, I like everybody in it... But *Taxi Driver* is really Paul Schrader's," the filmmaker once said. "We interpreted it. Paul Schrader gave the script to me because he saw *Mean Streets* and liked Bob in it and liked me as a director."

A film critic-turned-filmmaker (he was first lured into the world of movies by legendary critic Pauline Kael), Schrader had become obsessed with the character of Travis Bickle in the early 1970s. In the midst of personal crisis, Schrader identified with his troubled creation. "I was in a very dark place ... sort of in a desperate place, and this character was starting to take over my life," Schrader said in 2012. "I felt I had to write him so I wouldn't become him. I was not a screenwriter at that time, I was a film critic. But I wrote this as a script rather than as a novel because I knew scripts. I had been living in my car and drifting around,

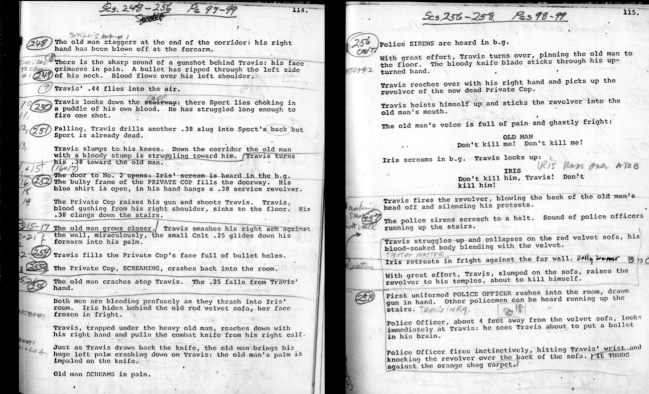

ABOVE: Paul Schrader's screenplay for *Taxi Driver*, complete with Scorsese's shooting notes.

and I was in the hospital, at the age of 26. When I was in the hospital, this metaphor occurred to me of the taxicab, this idea of this man in this metal coffin floating through the sewers of the city, who seems to be in the middle of society but in fact is desperately alone."

Scorsese, who was introduced to Schrader by mutual friend Brian De Palma while working on *Mean Streets*, could relate to the alienation coursing through the script even before reading it. "I felt close to the character by way of Dostoevsky," Scorsese once said. "I had always wanted to do a movie of *Notes from the Underground*," the author's 1864 novella written in the form of faux-memoir by its central character, an unnamed outcast. "I mentioned that to Paul and he said, 'Well, this is what I have: *Taxi Driver*,' and I said, 'Great, this is it.'"

ABOVE: Paul Schrader in 1978 around the time of *Taxi Driver*'s release.

III. GODDESS & WHORE

To understand the point of *Taxi Driver*'s violent finale, it's important to interpret correctly Scorsese's motivations for making the film. Although critics would soon embrace *Taxi Driver* for its political subtext, specifically its commentary on the country's disenchantment in the wake of Watergate, Scorsese insisted that his interest in the material was more personal. "I had to make that movie," he once said. "Not so much because of the social statement it makes, but because of its feeling about things, including things I don't like to admit to myself."

For Scorsese, it is Travis's unrequited love for Cybill Shepherd's Betsy that, in part, drives the story to its bloody climax. "The best way is to start with a character and then put him through scenes, through conflicts, that illustrate your theme," Scorsese explained. "When Travis falls in love with a woman, he can't admit he wants to make love to her... The movie deals with sexual repression, so there's a lot of talk but no sex, lovemaking, no nudity. If the audience saw nudity, it would work like a release valve and the tension that's been building up would be dissolved. The valve in *Taxi Driver* is not released until Travis finally lets loose and starts shooting."

That sexual repression was a response to the religious upbringing both Scorsese and Schrader had. (Scorsese was raised Catholic, while Schrader grew up in a Calvinist home.) In a 1976 interview, Scorsese noted that the characters in his films suffer from a "goddess-whore complex. You're raised to worship women, but you don't know how to approach them on a human level, on a sexual level. That's the thing with Travis … the girl he falls for, the Cybill Shepherd character, it's really important that she's blonde, a blue-eyed goddess."

As for Iris, Scorsese added, "She has the candles burning in her bedroom, she's like a saint to him. He can't imagine these pimps treating her the way they do. Before he goes to avenge her, it's almost like he cleanses himself, like in *The Virgin Spring* when Max von Sydow scourges himself with the branches before he goes out to avenge his daughter's death." (In the same interview, Schrader revealed, "We actually had that [*Virgin Spring*] shot in the movie, and we took it out. Travis whips himself with a towel before he goes out with his guns. We took it out because it looked a little forced and unnatural.")

BELOW: Jodie Foster, Robert De Niro, and Martin Scorsese on the set of *Taxi Driver*.

BELOW: Robert De Niro and Cybill Shepherd. "I never wanted it to end," she once said about the experience of making the movie. "It was just magic, like we were stealing it. I had the same feeling on [*The Last*] *Picture Show*, too. When they were both over, I just wept."

SEXUAL VIOLENCE

Taxi Driver paints an ugly picture of 1970s New York City. A Vietnam vet, Travis returns home and takes a job as a cab driver to make use of his insomniac hours. As he makes his way through the city at night he encounters its scum firsthand, from the pimps and hookers to the disturbingly calm psychopath (played by Scorsese, below right with De Niro), who frequently appears in cameo roles in his movies) who's planning to kill his philandering wife.

Disgusted by what he sees, Travis turns to Senator Palantine, the presidential candidate, and Betsy (below left), the "blue-eyed Goddess" who works for Palantine, who seem to be above the muck. But Betsy (unsurprisingly) spurns Travis's attentions after he takes her on a date to a hard-core porn show, and Travis loses his faith, returning to the dark thoughts, the loneliness, and the isolation that haunt him.

The violence that Betsy's rejection precipitates—first in his failed assassination attempt on Palantine (bottom), and then in the hotel—can be seen as the release that Travis never achieves sexually, or an act of hypermasculinity, with violence and killing as the acts that, to quote Scorsese, "take macho to its logical conclusion."

TOP & ABOVE: Scenes from the ultraviolent *The Wild Bunch*.

ABOVE: Director Sam Peckinpah on the set of *The Wild Bunch*.

IV. VIOLENCE & ANTIVIOLENCE

As a model for the type of response Scorsese wanted from *Taxi Driver*'s violent resolution, the filmmaker looked at Sam Peckinpah's 1969 revisionist Western *The Wild Bunch*, which begins and ends with superb, grim shoot-outs.

Fighting back against critics who at the time charged him with glorifying violence in *The Wild Bunch*, Peckinpah once declared, "Actually, it's an antiviolence film… [The violence] is ugly, brutalizing, and bloody fucking awful. It's not fun and games and cowboys and Indians—it's a terrible, ugly thing. And yet there's a certain response that you get from it, an excitement, because we're all violent people, we have violence within us. Violence is part of life and I don't think we can bury our heads in the sand and ignore it. It's important to understand it and the reason people seem to need violence vicariously."

Much like Peckinpah, Scorsese was surprised and a bit horrified by audiences' visceral reaction to Travis's killing spree. "I was disturbed by that," he said in 1990. "It wasn't done with that intent. You can't stop people from taking it that way. What can you do? And you can't stop people from getting an exhilaration from violence, because that's human, very much the same way as you get an exhilaration from the violence in *The Wild Bunch*. But the exhilaration in the violence at the end of *The Wild Bunch* and the violence that's in *Taxi Driver*—because

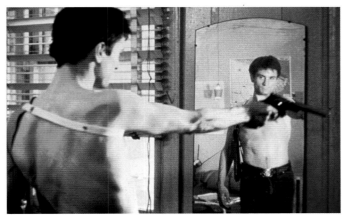

TOP & ABOVE: Travis Bickle practices his moves.

CRITIQUE OF MACHISMO

Despite its expression of masculine aggression, the *Taxi Driver* shoot-out eviscerates rather than celebrates such violent behavior. In part, the viewer senses this by the intentionally clumsy staging of the sequence. Instead of being dynamically edited, there's a bluntness to the cuts, Travis lurching from victim to victim with a gracelessness that underlines his desperate, determined mindset. The bullet wounds are ghastly, and the screams of pain are agonizing, with one innocent bystander, whose fingers have just been shot off, yelling, "I'll kill you!" over and over in shock and horror. Everything in the sequence deemphasizes Travis's seemingly heroic deed.

When Scorsese first read *Taxi Driver*, he thought of his own lonely childhood but also the lessons about masculinity he observed as a boy. "You grow up in a neighborhood where what a 'man' is, quote unquote, is a guy who can go into a room and slam some people around and win, like in a Schwarzenegger film," he said in *Conversations with Scorsese*. "But on the other hand, I heard my father say different things about what a man is; that had to do with being morally strong."

Consequently, *Taxi Driver* is a film about wrestling with those two extremes: aggression and civility; brute force and calm reason. "That's my question for most of my pictures," Scorsese said. "What is a man, and what is a hero? Does might make right? Or is it somebody who makes everybody reason things out and work it out? I think that's harder. Hit somebody long enough, they're going to stop. It works. For a while."

it's shot a certain way, and I know how it's shot, because I shot it and designed it—is also in the creation of that scene; in the editing, in the camera moves, in the use of music and the use of sound effects, and in the movement within the frame of the characters."

Still, Scorsese refused to accept that he was promoting violence, and indeed he talks of how the movie's violence is only a part of what sticks in the mind. "I was in China in '84 and a young man from Mongolia talked to me at length about *Taxi Driver*, about the loneliness. That's why the film seems to be something that people keep watching over and over. It's not the shoot-'em-out at the end."

V. THE SHOOT-OUT

The shoot-out scene is memorable not only for its violence, but also for a sense of ambiguity in it. This ambiguity pervades the whole movie, largely due to Schrader's refusal to shine any solid light on Travis's past or motivations—the viewer can only guess, follow clues, and interpret why Travis behaves the way he does. In this scene, the ambiguity comes from the combination of a gritty realism with stylization that elevates it to the dreamlike (or perhaps, more accurately, the nightmarish).

Through a combination of techniques, Scorsese conveys the horror and ugliness of the situation, as well as the deranged state of mind of its protagonist. Partly, this is due to De Niro's performance, combined with the way Scorsese shot it. Travis wades in as a hero saving Iris, but it's hard to view the scene in a heroic light. The murders are not perfectly executed—Travis is shot almost straight away—and the wild and clumsy violence is emphasized by disorienting camera angles, which also highlight the dark, claustrophobic corridors and stairwell of the seedy hotel. There's also the slow-motion factor: the violent scenes were shot in 48 frames to the second, double the usual 24, so when this is projected at the usual speed the action comes out in slow motion. Scorsese explained this decision:

"[We] wanted him to look almost like a monster, a robot, King Kong coming to save Fay Wray. Another thing: all of the close-ups of De Niro where he isn't talking were shot 48 frames to the second—to draw out and exaggerate his reactions. What an actor, to look so great up against a technique like that! I shot

ABOVE & RIGHT: Travis Bickle on his killing spree. Scorsese shot the violence in 48 frames per second so that it would play out slower, emphasizing the monstrosity of Travis's actions.

all those shots myself, to see for myself what kind of reaction we were getting."

The lack of music through this sequence is one of the brilliant aesthetic decisions that draw the horror of the scene to its full potential—the repeated cries of "I'll kill you! I'll kill you!" and Iris's whimpers stark and unavoidable against a backdrop of silence. But some of the decisions were made purely for practical reasons: the color in this scene was desaturated in order to bring the movie's rating down from an X to an R. The filmmaker says this was "just something I pulled out of a hat" but he was pleased with it:

"Actually I wanted the whole picture to be that way... It took us some doing, but I liked it a lot. It gave it more of a tabloid feel. Maybe more of the film should have looked like that."

THE OVERHEAD SHOT

The climatic sequence ends with a chilling overhead shot of the carnage Travis has wrought in his killing spree, the characters (whether dead or alive) all frozen motionless (below). It provides the audience with a moment to catch its breath while recoiling at the violence that's just been unleashed.

The task of executing the shot fell to cinematographer Michael Chapman.

"Marty loves dollies, Marty loves to move the camera around and around and around, all the time," Chapman once said. "And I had been working in the movies in New York for years and knew the crews and things there. And by accident the town was very slow when we started *Taxi Driver*. And I got together, because of that fortuitous circumstance, a very, very good crew."

When it came time to figure out the shoot-out sequence's overhead shot, Chapman remembered thinking, "Well, the only thing you can do is cut a hole in the floor of the next apartment upstairs."

"It was an old abandoned building and I drew a line where I wanted the opening and we just cut the ceiling out," Chapman recalled. "Crews, if they're good, are a lot smarter than some people think they are, and they respond to something unusual if it is amusing... A good crew can be extraordinarily sophisticated about movies without having any theoretical background for it. They just are from doing it. And they got challenged and turned on by Marty."

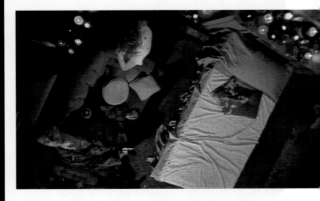

ABOVE: Alan Ladd in *Shane*.

ABOVE: Emeric Pressburger and Michael Powell.

TOP: *The Red Shoes*.

VI. BORROWING FROM THE BEST

In 1984, cinematographer Michael Chapman said of *Taxi Driver*, "[A]s far as a specific visual style, I don't know that we ever decided anything. We looked at a lot of movies beforehand. Lots and lots of movies; I can't even remember them all. That's the wonderful thing about Marty; he sees all movies and we looked at things that didn't have a hope of having anything to do with *Taxi Driver*. Things that were in no way relevant and then things that were obviously relevant like New York movies, film noir, *Sweet Smell of Success*, and things like that. Strangely we looked at a lot of black-and-white. But we looked at all sorts of movies and that was wonderful because it just made us sort of at ease with each other and confident that when we were talking about something we were talking about the same thing."

During a 1998 interview with Roger Ebert, Scorsese demonstrated his encyclopedic knowledge of film when describing the variety of cinematic antecedents that went into his conception of *Taxi Driver*'s look.

"There are several shots in *Taxi Driver* that are inspired by *Shane*," Scorsese began. "It's homage—the self-consciousness of saying, hey, here's a little nudge in the ribs to François Truffaut; that's a nudge to Federico Fellini; that's one to George Stevens; that's one to John Ford. You find yourself looking at old films a lot. The Hitchcock pictures I like looking at repeatedly, repeatedly, repeatedly. Very often without the sound. The Powell-Pressburger films, John Ford, Welles of course. What happens is that you find, through these images, a way of writing with the camera that stays in your mind.

ABOVE: Director Alfred Hitchcock on the set of *The Wrong Man*.

LEFT: Henry Fonda in *The Wrong Man*.

"*The Wrong Man* by Hitchcock has more to do with the camera movements in *Taxi Driver* than any other picture I can think of. It's such a heavy influence because of the sense of guilt and paranoia. Look at the scenes where Henry Fonda has to go back to the bank with the police and just walk up and down while the tellers look at him. They're deciding a man's fate. And watch the camera moves. Or the use of color in Michael Powell and Emeric Pressburger's *The Red Shoes*. I think there's that kind of … influencing. It's not necessarily direct stealing. Each film is interlocked with so many other films. You can't get away. Whatever you do now that you think is new was already done in 1913."

SUMMARY OF TECHNIQUE

1. A LACK OF CHOREOGRAPHY

By avoiding polished camera moves and through electrifying editing during the scene, *Taxi Driver* undercuts Travis Bickle's heroic narrative, putting the focus on the bloodshed and brutality rather than on the inherent excitement of an action sequence.

2. THE OVERHEAD SHOT

The slow panning shot that surveys the deaths from above gives us what's known as a "god's eye view." Such overhead shots are incorporated to flatten the action or to place the viewer above the action, so as to give us a feeling of superiority to what we're watching. In *Taxi Driver*, Scorsese utilizes the technique for its unabashed starkness, forcing us to ponder the violence from a clinical, unsentimental, sober perspective.

3. SUBVERTING EXPECTATIONS

One of the most powerful filmic effects is to create an expectation in an audience and then deliver upon that promise, but with a twist. In *Taxi Driver*, Travis Bickle's slow-building anger leads us to believe that he will eventually go berserk. But while he does just that in this final sequence, Scorsese, De Niro, and writer Paul Schrader conspire to surprise us. Travis "rescues" Iris, but he kills innocent bystanders along the way, their agony and suffering impossible to shake. And instead of acting heroically, Travis is upsettingly methodical, almost psychopathically calm during the shootings, giving us nothing to connect to. We have arrived at the sequence we were expecting, but its emotional payoff is completely unexpected.

THE LAST WALTZ
1978

CINEMATOGRAPHER:
Michael Chapman

EDITORS:
Jan Roblee
Yeu-Bun Yee

PRODUCTION DESIGNER:
Boris Leven

PRINCIPAL PERFORMERS:
Rick Danko
Levon Helm
Garth Hudson
Richard Manuel
Robbie Robertson

SCENE:
The Band performs "The Night They Drove
Old Dixie Down"

03

I. INTRODUCTION

Rock 'n' roll has been central to Martin Scorsese's movies from the beginning. And in fact it was the filmmaker's scrupulous use of pop and rock songs on the soundtrack to *Mean Streets* that opened the door to his most famous celebration of the music that helped shape his generation.

The quintet known as The Band started out as a backing band for Ronnie Hawkins, a rockabilly singer of the late 1950s and early 60s. But they soon went their own way, working as a recording and touring act before signing up to support Bob Dylan on the road and in the studio. Known as The Hawks, they later changed their name to The Band as a response to all the overly colorful, psychedelic-sounding groups of the time with their trippy, flowery names.

Led by Robbie Robertson, The Band produced a series of indelible albums, including 1968's *Music from Big Pink* and 1969's *The Band*, but by the mid-'70s they were running out of gas. Tired of touring, The Band decided to call it quits, but Robertson wanted to throw one last blowout concert. And he was interested in having it filmed, although he was unhappy with the concert documentaries of the time. Robertson said, "I watched music on television and in movies, and I asked myself, 'Is this the line of work I'm in?' Because if it is, I find it embarrassing, obnoxious, and very poorly done—so less than listening to music in my imagination."

But Robertson found the right artist to chronicle his group's last show in Scorsese. Recalled the director, "I was kind of seduced into it by Jonathan Taplin, the producer of *Mean Streets*, who called me when I was doing *New York, New York* and said a lot of the rock people were watching the film … He said he wanted to have a screening for a few friends, including Robbie Robertson." The two men immediately hit it off, and Robertson proposed a concert film that would feature not just The Band but some of their famous musician friends, including Bob Dylan, Joni Mitchell, Neil Diamond, Neil Young, and Van Morrison. Scorsese couldn't resist.

The film of that final show, *The Last Waltz*, is considered one of the great rock documentaries. Shot during The Band's farewell concert at San Francisco's Winterland Ballroom on Thanksgiving Day of November 25, 1976, the movie didn't hit

theaters for another two years. Because Scorsese has so many narrative masterworks to his name, *The Last Waltz* is almost underrated in his canon. But its evocation of masculine relationships and its clear affection for rock music mark it as a quintessential Scorsese film. These concerns are expressed explicitly in the documentary's superb presentation of The Band's signature track, "The Night They Drove Old Dixie Down."

ABOVE: The Band relaxing in 1968. Robbie Robertson is at the far right. Drummer-singer Levon Helm is center.

II. THE VISION

Initially, Scorsese had modest expectations for *The Last Waltz*, planning to shoot it on economical handheld 16mm cameras. But then he decided to get more ambitious. He had been a supervising editor on *Woodstock*, the seminal documentary of the titular 1969 concert, which had been shot on 16mm. So why not use a larger format for this send-off to The Band? The specs soon escalated. "In the end I came up with the idea of shooting it in 35mm, with full synch sound and seven cameras," he later recalled. "The Band were paying for the raw stock, while the cameramen and I would get a percentage if the picture was ever made, and in the meantime we'd enjoy the show."

The decision helped give *The Last Waltz* a warm, full-bodied glow, appropriate to the nostalgic tenor of the night, as well as The Band's roots-rock songs, which frequently referenced failed loves and the occasional historic event. Scorsese dove into preproduction, working out a massive script based on the group's proposed set list. "What I did was give him the information on all the material," Robertson recalled in 1982. "I would let him know how the introduction to the thing went, what instrument it was, and then he had all the lyrics to the songs and I would say who took the solo, or how it was traded off. So, what he did, he had this thing made up where, on the side of the page, he wrote in all the [lighting], the

BELOW: Robbie Robertson, frontman for The Band, talks with director Martin Scorsese during the making of *The Last Waltz*.

BOTTOM, BELOW, & OPPOSITE LEFT: For *The Last Waltz*, The Band performed alongside an array of special guests, including Joni Mitchell and Neil Young (below), Eric Clapton (bottom), and Bob Dylan (opposite).

camera moves that he was going to try his best to get during the concert… [W]hen there's an audience there and everything, you can't just do whatever the hell you want."

The Band's drummer and occasional lead vocalist Levon Helm once noted, "Scorsese and Robertson produced a 150-page shooting script so detailed that lighting cues were matched to chord changes in individual songs."

It also helped that Scorsese loved The Band's songs. "He knows the music as well as I know it," Robertson said. "Obscure songs on the fourth album, fifth song on the second side—he knows the words to the third verse."

NO REHEARSALS, NO AUDIENCE

Some concert filmmakers will "cheat" by shooting dress rehearsals, inserting some of that footage alongside the actual live performance that occurs later. According to Helm, Scorsese watched rehearsals but didn't film them, presumably wanting to stick to the actual concert. Additionally, Scorsese declined to film the audience during *The Last Waltz*, which is still a pretty common occurrence in concert movies. "I had the feeling that the movie audience could become more involved with the concert if we concentrated on the stage," he told the *Village Voice* in 1978. "Besides, after *Woodstock*"—which featured plenty of crowd shots—"who wants to see the audience anymore?"

Scorsese tapped *Taxi Driver* cinematographer Michael Chapman to shoot the film, but he also brought on other heralded cameramen, including Vilmos Zsigmond (*The Deer Hunter, Close Encounters of the Third Kind*) and László Kovács (*Easy Rider*), to be additional directors of photography. "The form of it was important to me—the camera movement to music, the editing, capturing the live performances," Scorsese told critic Richard Schickel. As opposed to the *cinéma vérité* documentaries of the 1960s, "This was staged, more studied in a way, much more planned out."

ABOVE: Drummer Levon Helm performs during *The Last Waltz*.

ABOVE: Robertson and Helm in a more relaxed moment.

III. THE SONG & THE SINGING DRUMMER

That sense of careful staging plays out all over *The Last Waltz*, but it's particularly notable in "The Night They Drove Old Dixie Down." The ballad, from the album *The Band*, documents the waning days of the American Civil War as the South's defeat is all but assured.

After The Band's breakup, Helm accused Robertson of hogging the songwriting credit for many of the group's songs, and in his memoir, *This Wheel's on Fire*, the drummer wrote, "Robbie and I worked on 'The Night They Drove Old Dixie Down' up in Woodstock. I remember taking him to the library so he could research the history and geography of the era for the lyrics and make [Confederate] General Robert E. Lee come out with all due respect…[W]e found if we halved the beat we could lay the lyrics in a different place, and the pulse would be easier to move to, more danceable."

On *The Band*, "Dixie Down" has a funereal grandeur, a wounded resignation. In *The Last Waltz*, those emotions are only amplified. Despite the

addition of a horn section, "Dixie Down" still cuts to the bone in the film version. Scorsese focused his cameras on Helm behind the drum kit as the musician passionately intoned (and ennobled) the words of a battered Southern soldier weary of war.

Resisting handheld cameras, Scorsese shot the song with a smooth, melancholy grace, a slow, gliding tracking shot across the stage making The Band look like the heroic, weary road warriors that Robertson envisioned them to be. The song is sung by Helm, but the cameras cut back and forth between him and Robertson, unconsciously underlining a tension between the band members.

"By the time *The Last Waltz* came up, it was no secret our collaboration and … the quality of our music had suffered," Helm said in 2007. "I didn't hear us getting better. I heard us, you know, doing albums with old songs that we liked, as opposed to getting in and really trying to grow a fresh crop of songs. And so I certainly didn't want to end The Band. *The Last Waltz*, you know, didn't set right

ABOVE RIGHT: Levon Helm works the drums during *The Last Waltz*.

RIGHT: Robbie Robertson wielding his guitar at The Band's farewell show.

with me. But, you know, there comes a time when we all want to move on, and that's what we did."

Helm's reluctance and ambivalence about The Band's end is reflected in his performance of "Dixie Down." Singing a song about collapse and failure, he's defiant and vibrant, almost in opposition to the scene's tear-stained wistfulness. By comparison, Robertson, at the front of the stage and not trapped behind a kit, has an almost beatific glow, the warrior artist taking his final bow.

The drummer never liked the movie and its worship of Robertson. When Helm went to see *The Last Waltz* before its opening, he was stunned. "For two hours we watched as the camera focused almost exclusively on Robbie Robertson," he later wrote, "long and loving close-ups of his heavily made-up face and expensive haircut. The film was edited so it looked like Robbie was conducting the band with expansive waves of his guitar neck. The muscles on his neck stood out like cords when he sang so powerfully into his switched-off microphone."

IV. SHOOTING MUSIC

With Scorsese at the helm, *The Last Waltz* was never going to be merely another concert film. Previous rock documentaries had largely been filmed on the cheap, using material they were given. Extensively storyboarded by Scorsese and Robertson, and using seven of the greatest cameramen of the time—yet edited purely from the performance and retaining the authenticity that was so important to rock—*The Last Waltz* presents an incredibly unique and daring hybrid between concert and movie. Filmed on a stage set designed by Boris Leven before an audience of

5,000 in San Francisco's Winterland Ballroom, *The Last Waltz* way a grand production in every way.

Leven had worked with Scorsese on *New York, New York*, and been acclaimed for his work on *Giant*, *The Sound of Music*, and *West Side Story*. The set he created for *The Last Waltz* included three huge chandeliers and many elements that were borrowed from the San Francisco Opera, lending an extravagant *belle époque* backdrop to the performances. A rolling camera track was built for the moving camera, and stands were set right into the Winterland's

foundations when the floor proved a little unstable. Importantly, Leven's lighting was designed for the camera, so that in the movie, the artists are not washed out by harsh spotlights typical of concert lighting, but captured beautifully.

The set design, the ambition of the endeavor, the special guests, are all impressive—yet the film is personal and warm. *The Last Waltz* was, after all, a farewell performance, and Scorsese's intimacy with the band and the music meant that he shot with sensitivity to the emotional side of the event. Helm may have resented Scorsese's martyr treatment, but nonetheless *The Last Waltz*'s sense of beautiful exhaustion is rendered warmly. This was a new side of the filmmaker's personality. Letting shots linger rather than cutting frantically from angle to angle in a desperate attempt to replicate the energy of a rock show, Scorsese was reaching toward the elegiac after making a few films emphasizing the dark and the edgy of the American subconscious.

A BEAUTIFUL FRIENDSHIP

The Last Waltz was a new way for Scorsese to explore male friendships, but in "Dixie Down" he was clearly siding with Robertson's doomed poet. That's hardly surprising since the two men had become close friends, Robertson even moving into Scorsese's Los Angeles home for a time, after he and his wife split. As Scorsese's ex-girlfriend Sandy Weintraub famously told Hollywood journalist Peter Biskind in *Easy Riders, Raging Bulls*, "It was a shame that Marty wasn't gay. The best relationship he ever had was probably with Robbie." The two men collaborated on the editing of *The Last Waltz*, working throughout the night and phoning co-editor Yeu-Bun Yee (who was also an editor on *Woodstock*) at all hours with ideas.

Profoundly, Scorsese identified with the finality of *The Last Waltz*, believing that his own career was near the end. Juggling *New York, New York* and *The Last Waltz* while suffering from a drug problem, he felt used up, spent. "I'm slowing down," he confessed to the *Village Voice* at the time. "I mean, I have projects, but none of them are ready yet. They'll have to wait until I am ready or else they won't get done. I want to get away from big budgets. I don't know what I'm going to do next. But I can't keep up the kind of thing I've been doing the past two years… It's like The Band—just because The Band broke up doesn't mean the music's over. It's just a hiatus, a stopping, before something different, more complex, the next step."

LEFT & ABOVE: The grand set designed by Boris Leven.

ABOVE: Martin Scorsese and Robbie Robertson.

V. THE UNEXPECTED

As smoothly choreographed as *The Last Waltz* seems, its shooting turned out to be more haphazard than Scorsese had intended. The filmmaker had hoped that his extensive shooting script would prepare him for every eventuality. "[Cinematographer] Mike Chapman executed all the lighting cues," Scorsese told writer Mary Pat Kelly for *Martin Scorsese: The First Decade*. "And I told the cameramen where to be. The notations [in the shooting script] were just guides—but I had everything written in, dolly shots, everything. I had it all down beforehand. So if one camera would go out of film, for example, say Camera Two would be out of film, and he was on the keyboard, and I'd know where Camera Five was, I'd say, 'Can you switch over and get a shot of the keyboard? Camera Two is going out of film.' Bang—it was like a football game, like television directing."

Rock 'n' roll rarely operates in such an orderly fashion, however. As Scorsese noted, "[O]nce The Band started playing you couldn't hear anybody [on the walkie-talkies]. But eventually, in spite of all the screaming, the cameras picked it up and once I saw the rushes I realized we had a movie."

"I'm very proud of it, I'm very proud I had a chance to do it," Chapman has said about *The Last Waltz*. "There's never been … a concert film as good as it since. And that's in large part—I mean, we did a very good job and we really thought it out and planned it out—because The Band was the intellectual elite of rock 'n' roll. Those songs are wonderful songs… I think, as much as possible, [we] did them justice."

But there was also some behind-the-scenes wizardry that was required. John Simon, The Band's longtime producer who served as *The Last Waltz*'s musical director, revealed that post-production tweaking was necessary for the concert film's sound mix. This is hardly novel—plenty of concert movies and live albums go through a similar process of polishing—but Simon noted that he had to focus on "playing mistakes, out-of tune singing [and] bad horn-balance in the remote truck." One portion didn't need to be fixed, though: according to Simon, "Only Levon's part was retained in its entirety."

ABOVE: All of the sound had to be re-dubbed in post production—except for Levon Helm's parts.

ABOVE: Neil Young, behind Robbie Robertson, also required FX wizardry to edit a large lump of cocaine from his nostril.

SUMMARY OF TECHNIQUE

1. EMPHASIS ON PERFORMANCE

Where other concert films cut away to the crowd to create a sense of excitement, in *The Last Waltz*, cameras are firmly trained on the performers, giving us a more intimate vantage point of a rock band in the midst of their craft. Because of this, it's easy to develop a bond with The Band and their special guests since we feel like we're up there on the stage with them.

2. CREATING WARMTH

To achieve the bittersweet, nostalgic tone he was seeking, Scorsese utilizes slow camera moves, warm lighting, and deliberate cuts. Consequently, *The Last Waltz* has an elegiac, unhurried pace, making The Band's final concert feel like a regal pageant rather than a raucous barnburner.

3. PREPARATION

Although Scorsese's elaborate shooting script became difficult to execute once the concert started and the walkie-talkie communication was drowned out by the noise, *The Last Waltz* nonetheless benefited from the preparations he and his cameramen had gone through. Even when a sophisticated strategy hits a snag when it comes to shoot, that doesn't mean that the pre-planning won't still pay off.

4. PLENTY OF COVERAGE

By using seven cameras, Scorsese had several angles of each performance, which gave him and his editors options for the final film. Concerts have a degree of unpredictability to them, but Scorsese gave himself some flexibility by positioning cameramen all over the stage and the venue, which allowed the individual members of The Band to shine depending on the song.

RAGING BULL
1980

SCREENPLAY:
Paul Schrader and Mardik Martin (Based on
Raging Bull: My Story by Jake LaMotta with
Joseph Carter and Peter Savage)

CINEMATOGRAPHER:
Michael Chapman

EDITOR:
Thelma Schoonmaker

PRINCIPAL SCENE ACTORS:
Robert De Niro (Jake LaMotta)
Johnny Barnes (Sugar Ray Robinson)

SCENE:
The St. Valentine's Day Massacre

04

I. INTRODUCTION

Martin Scorsese's films demonstrate how brutality can be transformed into art, never more so than in *Raging Bull*. A gruesome portrait of self-destructive prizefighter Jake LaMotta, the film won Robert De Niro his second Oscar, an acknowledgment of the doomed savagery the actor brought to the role.

Comparing *Raging Bull* to other boxing films like *City for Conquest* and *Body and Soul*, cinematographer Michael Chapman commented, "Bobby De Niro is a better fighter than any of those [other actors]. He looks and moves like a fighter. He has the punches and convincingness of a fighter, much more so. With [James] Cagney or [John] Garfield, you always have a sense that they are actors portraying a fighter. But Bobby is really a fighter. He spent a year not doing anything, just working out every day, obsessively."

That preparation paid off in *Raging Bull*'s boxing scenes, specifically its final one. Throughout the film, LaMotta's greatest nemesis is Sugar Ray Robinson. Near the story's conclusion, the two middleweight titans square off one last time. LaMotta loses; more accurately, he is destroyed by Robinson's flurry of punches. The scene is a tapestry of blood, sadness, and masochism. It can be hard to watch, partly because the emotions of the moment are so painful.

Inasmuch as *Taxi Driver* can be said to be Paul Schrader's movie, *Raging Bull* is De Niro's film. It was the actor who convinced Scorsese to take on the project in the first place. Ultimately, the project turned out to be a gift to Scorsese. Despite mixed reviews and a less-than-explosive opening at the box office, it would be nominated for eight Academy Awards and go on to win two—Best Actor for De Niro's performance, and Thelma Schoonmaker's first Oscar for editing. It might have been passed over for Best Picture, but it secured Scorsese's reputation as a filmmaker.

ABOVE & OPPSITE: Robert De Niro as Jake LaMotta.

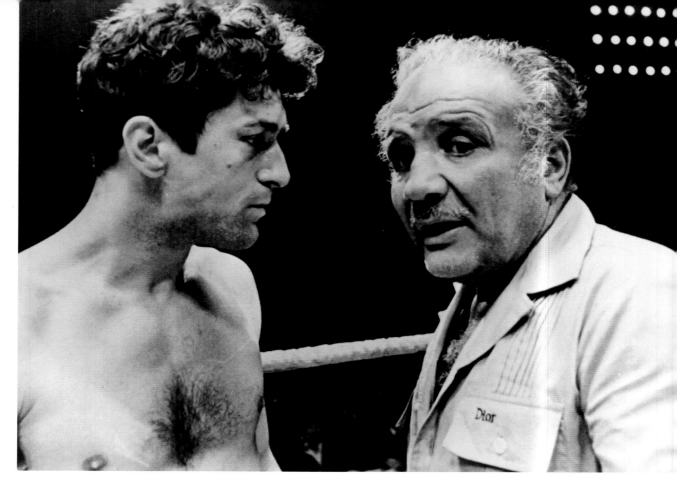

II. THE DE NIRO EFFECT

Raging Bull was the fourth collaboration between
Scorsese and De Niro, and their relationship was by
now as complex and intimate as family. "By the time
we were doing *Raging Bull* we were like brothers, in
the best and worst sense," Scorsese has said. "You
know, we had the same trust, but at the same time,
there were annoyances."

One of De Niro's annoyances was that Scorsese
wasn't particularly interested in doing a movie about
LaMotta. Before the two men worked on *Taxi Driver*
and *New York, New York*, De Niro had insisted that
LaMotta's life would be cinematic. The actor had
received LaMotta's memoir, *Raging Bull: My Story*,
while getting ready to do *1900*, Bernardo Bertolucci's

TOP: Robert De Niro confers with Jake LaMotta.

ABOVE: The real Jake LaMotta and Sugar Ray Robinson
slug it out in the ring.

epic. By all accounts the book was no great work of literature, but the actor saw something in it. "There was something about it—a strong thrust, a portrait of a direct man without complications," De Niro explained about his fascination with the book. But Scorsese had no real interest in the film at the time; he was not interested in boxing, to begin with, and he was exhausted by the poor reception of *New York, New York* and his efforts on *The Last Waltz*, which had followed immediately.

But De Niro was determined that Scorsese would be the one to make the film, and he was not going to take no for an answer. When Scorsese finally came around on *Raging Bull*, it was because of his personal struggles with drug abuse. In seriously poor health and ordered to stay in bed, Scorsese communicated with De Niro, who saw a connection between the director's physical and spiritual collapse and the one that afflicted LaMotta. (The boxer has been married seven times, battled alcoholism, and spent time in jail.) "I couldn't understand Bob's obsession with it, until, finally, I went through that rough period of my own," Scorsese told film critic, Richard Schickel. "I came out the other side and woke up one day alive ... still breathing."

Struggling with the screenplay, Scorsese and De Niro retired to a resort on St. Martin in the Caribbean, where together they worked out their vision for the film with a script that Paul Schrader had developed. It was during this period that the story became more and more stripped down. A key decision was leaving the characters' behavior unexplained. Scorsese observed that in his autobiography, LaMotta seems to be constantly analyzing himself. In contrast, the characters in *Raging Bull* can be understood only in terms of what they actually say and do, and this gives a purity to the pathos and evokes surprising empathy from the viewer toward the unpleasant LaMotta—particularly in the moment when he is destroyed by Sugar Ray in this painful fight scene.

BODY AND SOUL

Scorsese, who grew up asthmatic, didn't have any particular fondness for boxing. "I didn't know anything about boxing," the filmmaker once told critic Richard Schickel. "It was always one angle on TV or in the movie theaters, where they'd show the fights on the weekend. I didn't know what the hell was going on. It was sports, which took me out of the picture."

So, to prepare for *Raging Bull*, he studied boxing movies, taking special interest in *Body and Soul*, a 1947 film that starred John Garfield as a down-on-his-luck pugilist. The immersive boxing scenes, directed by Robert Rossen and shot by James Wong Howe, gave Scorsese ideas about how to film his own. Particularly noteworthy was that Howe had been filming on roller skates inside the ring to give a sense of documentary-like realism.

ABOVE: Stills from *Body and Soul*.

III. THE ACTOR'S METHOD

Robert De Niro was famous for his preparation for roles, and with *Raging Bull* he gained 60 pounds to portray LaMotta during his post-boxing career. But his relationship with Scorsese also granted him a great degree of latitude from the filmmaker that allowed him to take chances in the role.

"At times he'd say, 'Let me try something,' and I would trust him and say, 'Go ahead,'" Scorsese has said. "And I would generally like what he did so we would keep pushing each other in that way and it became that kind of collaboration. I knew that inevitably—especially if we were in a situation where we had to improvise something or we were in a situation and we had to roll with it and something happened by accident—I knew that he was the one person who would find the truth in the action."

Steven Spielberg explained De Niro and Scorsese's relationship to writer Andy Dougan as "something about Bobby being Marty's alter ego. Marty allows Bobby to do the violence, he allows Bobby to be the hitman so to speak. He allows Bobby to take the fall, lets Bobby go over the top and lose control so that Marty can remain in control. I think Bobby is just wonderful as a sort of extension of what Marty might have been if he hadn't been a filmmaker."

But as dedicated as De Niro was to his training and his close studying of LaMotta, the actor didn't feel any need to emulate the boxer's temperament. He wanted to understand the prizefighter—but he didn't want to become him, saying, "I'm not one of those actors who goes around in private giving off that macho thing. I lead a low-profile life. The world is full of guys who can't wait to come up to you in a bar and show you how tough they are. What Jake taught me was how to take punishment, but I'm not anxious to prove a point. I know I'm supposed to be the actor who carries his role over into private life. There is a small spillage, but I don't flip out."

SUGAR RAY

From 1942 to 1951, LaMotta and Robinson fought six times, with Robinson coming out the victor on five occasions. "I fought Sugar Ray so many times it's a wonder I didn't get diabetes," LaMotta would joke.

Scorsese depicts three of those fights in *Raging Bull*, with each man winning one of the first two. But the final bout, from 1951 and dubbed the "St. Valentine's Day Massacre"—because it occurred on February 14—is the most punishing on LaMotta, as Robinson assaults him with a vicious flurry of jabs and punches.

But where De Niro trained to capture LaMotta's essence, his co-star landed the role in a different way. Johnny Barnes grew up resembling Robinson, and even befriended the boxer's wife. Barnes said in 2005, "She loved that I looked like her husband. She'd tell people, 'He looks like my Sugar, all young again.'" An occasional actor, Barnes was a boxer for a time—he also spent years battling drug addiction—but in the late 1970s he landed the role of Robinson for Scorsese's film.

"Marty and Bob wanted the real thing, the most authentic people so the film would look real," *Raging Bull*'s casting director Cis Corman told the *Times*.

Unlike LaMotta, whom Scorsese and screenwriters Paul Schrader and Mardik Martin captured with nuance, Robinson is intentionally one-dimensional, an unknowable nemesis who's more lethal and intimidating because he's a cipher. And where *Raging Bull* continued to elevate De Niro's stardom, the movie failed to do much for Barnes, who tried unsuccessfully to launch a Sugar Ray Robinson biopic. Scorsese's movie was as close as he ever got.

"I always felt it was my destiny to play Robinson in his life story, and I still haven't given up that dream," said Barnes. "I still know that I'm the best man for that part … I always retained a certain amount of the role. Being associated with Sugar Ray doesn't bother me. He's always been a part of my life."

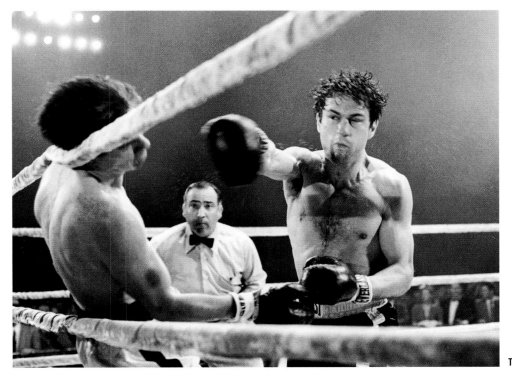

LEFT & OPPOSITE: De Niro threw himself into training for *Raging Bull*; by the time of the film he really could have been a contender.

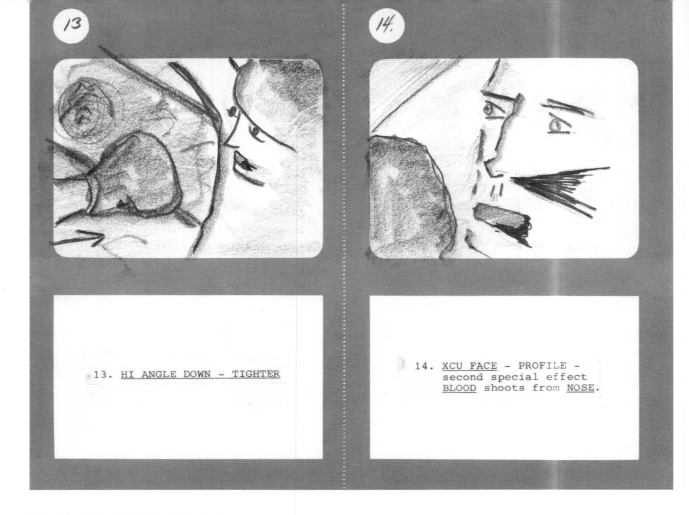

13. HI ANGLE DOWN - TIGHTER

14. XCU FACE - PROFILE -
second special effect
BLOOD shoots from NOSE.

IV. PLANNING THE SHOT

Inspired by the powerful fight scenes in *Body and Soul*, Scorsese and his cinematographer carefully mapped out their boxing scenes. "We spent more time on the fights than the whole rest of the movie," Chapman once admitted. "In terms of screen time, though, it doesn't play more than ten or fifteen minutes. So those scenes are very, very elaborate."

Scorsese drew his own storyboards for the film's boxing scenes. For the final bout between Jake LaMotta and Sugar Ray Robinson, in which LaMotta is savagely pummeled in the thirteenth round, the filmmaker drew inspiration from a twenty-year-old horror movie that was also shot in black-and-white, Alfred Hitchcock's *Psycho*.

"[T]he boxing scenes have a lot to do with the action sequences in my mind," Scorsese said. "All this editing and all this camera movement that I'd been exposed to for the past 25 years or 30 years came into play in those sequences, and Hitchcock had a lot to do with it, there's no doubt, particularly in designing the scene where Sugar Ray Robinson, in the third bout that they have, when LaMotta's on the ropes, looks up at him, and Sugar Ray comes in for the kill. And there's a kind of edited sequence of punishment that this character's taking. I based it on, shot by shot, the shower scene of *Psycho*. And so I designed it correspondingly, in a way. The glove corresponds to a knife. And so, we shot it that way."

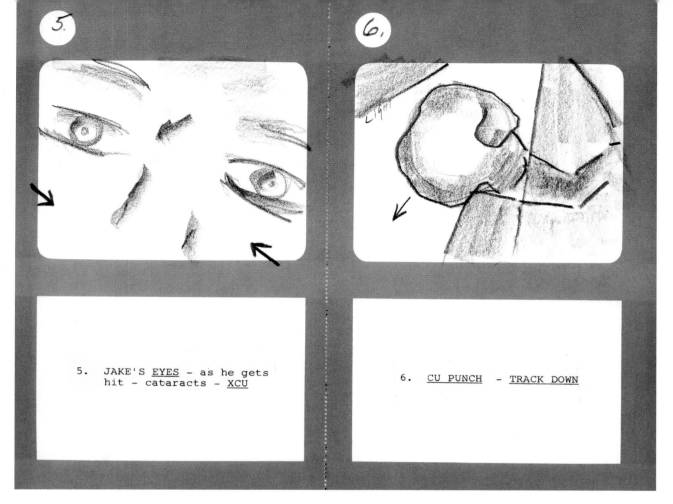

5. JAKE'S <u>EYES</u> - as he gets hit - cataracts - <u>XCU</u>

6. <u>CU PUNCH</u> - <u>TRACK DOWN</u>

ABOVE & OPPOSITE: Scorsese's storyboards for *Raging Bull*.

BELOW: Storyboards from Alfred Hitchcock's *Psycho*.

V. BLACK & WHITE

For all the lurid flowing of blood and sweat in its boxing scenes, *Raging Bull* is perhaps most striking because we don't see any colors. It's coincidence that LaMotta's autobiography opens with the line, "When my memories come back to me, I have the feeling that I'm watching an old film in black and white." The decision was made when, at an early screening, Michael Powell pointed out that the red gloves felt all wrong, when fights of that period were shown in black and white.

As a movie set in the 1940s and 50s, shooting in black and white makes aesthetic sense, evoking the screened fights of that period. The decision was agreed upon early in the process by Scorsese and cinematographer Michael Chapman.

"He just called me up and asked me if I wanted to shoot it in black and white," Chapman said. "I think perhaps Bobby De Niro wanted to do it in black and white also. I think it was a very wise decision. I think that if you are above a certain age, you tend to think that real movies are black and white anyway. I certainly do. I mean, the movies that formed me and that are

BELOW: Martin Scorsese and Robert De Niro compare notes.

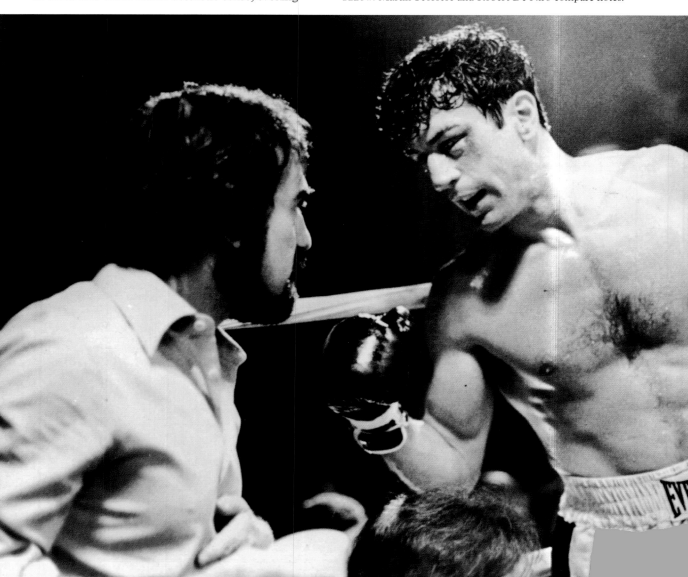

deepest in my unconscious are black and white, by and large. And certainly you think of fight movies in black-and-white… Anyone's memories of Jake LaMotta are black and white memories."

There was another practical explanation for Scorsese's choice: the director had been unhappy with color processing at the time. "The color has to mean something," he told an audience at the Santa Barbara Film Festival in 2012. "It's a very important element. And it was on a stock that, within five years, would go pink or magenta."

GOING IN PREPARED

Scorsese and Chapman weren't going to dive into shooting in black and white without preparing. They looked at press and tabloid shots and screened classic black-and-white films like *Sweet Smell of Success* (below) and *Double Indemnity* (bottom). The former, whose cinematography was also done by *Body and Soul*'s James Wong Howe, was cited by Martin Scorsese as the look he would like to reference, if to reference anything at all.

VI. A STYLIZED REALITY

The scene of Jake LaMotta's final confrontation with Sugar Ray Robinson is highly stylized, almost abstract, but not unrealistic. It was about creating a reality that was not historically inaccurate, but subordinate to the more important feeling and dramatic truth of the moment unfolding.

All kinds of visual trickery were employed to create this cinematic truth, many of which might not be noticeable on a surface level. The ring where this last fight takes place, for example, was larger than regulation size, and larger than other rings that were used during the film. Slow-motion photography is used, and Scorsese used flames beneath the camera lens, and smoke filling the arena, to produce a disorienting effect on the filmed environment.

Experimentation was not limited to visuals either, Frank Warner's innovative approach to sound for this sequence has been much lauded. "The sound on *Raging Bull* was particularly difficult because each punch, each camera click and each flashbulb was different," Scorsese recalled. "The sound effects were done by Frank Warner, who had worked on *Close Encounters of the Third Kind* and *Taxi Driver*. He used rifle shots and melon breaking." But sometimes no sound at all, as in the final bout, proved more devastating: "Silence, then suddenly the punch goes flying—whack!"

The blood was created using Hershey's chocolate and the iconic final image of the scene—a shot of blood dripping from one of the ropes—was inspired by something Scorsese had seen at an actual fight at Madison Square Garden that he attended while doing research. "I was in the fifth row from the front, and I saw the blood coming off the rope," he recalled. "As the next bout was announced, no one took any notice of it."

ABOVE & RIGHT: The copious blood in *Raging Bull* was created from Hershey's chocolate—just one example of the creative ingenuity that went on behind the scenes to give *Raging Bull* its visual power.

SUMMARY OF TECHNIQUE

1. NO COLOR
While using black and white can be a gimmick like any other device, *Raging Bull* utilizes a monochromatic look to superb effect, adding intensity to the violence and bloodshed. But it's also important to keep in mind that Scorsese also chose to shoot in black and white because he was unhappy with color processing at the time: creative choices are sometimes provoked by practical considerations.

2. GETTING CREATIVE
Scorsese and his team incorporated items like Hershey's chocolate to enhance their visuals —the blood in *Raging Bull*'s boxing scene doesn't look entirely realistic, but it feels real in a visceral way. By thinking abut the way it will come across visually, the film embraces realism while giving it an added force.

3. RESEARCH
One of the final boxing scene's greatest images—the shot of a blood-smeared rope encircling the ring—came about because Scorsese had observed such a moment at a boxing match. Sometimes, the best ideas and visuals are drawn directly from research into the world that a filmmaker is chronicling.

4. IDENTIFYING WITH THE MATERIAL
For years, Scorsese didn't share De Niro's passion for Jake LaMotta's story. It was only after the filmmaker had experienced some personal lows that he began to relate more to the boxer's spiritual exhaustion. Movies are far more than exercises in technical craftsmanship: some of the greatest films feel personal, the director communicating something universal and heartfelt directly to the audience. Look no further than *Raging Bull* as an example of how passion and skill can intertwine beautifully.

THE KING OF COMEDY

1982

SCREENPLAY:
Paul D. Zimmerman

CINEMATOGRAPHER:
Fred Schuler

EDITOR:
Thelma Schoonmaker

PRODUCTION DESIGNER:
Boris Leven

PRINCIPAL SCENE ACTOR:
Robert De Niro (Rupert Pupkin)

SCENE:
Rupert Pupkin's imaginary performance

05

I. INTRODUCTION

Alienation is a crucial theme in Martin Scorsese's films. Often, the director examines isolated, occasionally misanthropic souls in the context of dramas and psychological thrillers: *Taxi Driver*, *Raging Bull*, *Bringing Out the Dead*, *The Aviator*, *Shutter Island*. But for *The King of Comedy*, Scorsese provocatively switched gears, delivering a character study-cum-dark comedy. That stylistic alteration didn't make his movie's protagonist any more lovable, though.

As played by Robert De Niro, Rupert Pupkin is all sweaty faux-confidence. Where previous collaborations between De Niro and Scorsese found the two-time Oscar winner portraying sullen, emotionally bruised men, *The King of Comedy* made the character's neediness more explicit, more naked, more unseemly. An aspiring comic who longs to appear on the *Jerry Langford Show*, the nation's top late-night talk show and a launching pad for stand-ups, Rupert is clearly a deeply untalented, potentially unstable schmuck. But the film honors his hopelessly upbeat determination, and in the process the audience is treated to one of De Niro's most scabrous performances. The actor lays bare Rupert's awkward ambition, forcing us to look into the eyes of unqualified, irredeemable failure.

But the movie's highlight scene is one of its shortest. Running less than a minute, the moment depicts Rupert as he delivers his jokes in front of an adoring crowd. But, as we soon realize, there is no laughing throng, just a giant photo of a cheering audience stuck up on the wall. With a simple camera move pulling slowing away from the back of Rupert, Scorsese paints a disturbing, claustrophobic portrait of a psychotic mind. We're not sure whether to laugh, shake our head, or recoil in recognition of our own secret self-delusions. The whole of *The King of Comedy* is encompassed in that shot.

OPPOSITE: Robert De Niro as Rupert Pupkin in *The King of Comedy*.

II. THE INITIAL RESISTANCE

Though ostensibly a satire, *The King of Comedy* doesn't allow Rupert Pupkin to be a simple laughing stock, a defenseless punching bag for the audience to pummel from a safe distance. That was by design; a reflection of the filmmakers' own complicated feelings toward this struggling entertainer.

"It's so grim," Scorsese once said of *The King of Comedy*. "For me it's about how my fantasies and De Niro's fantasies have come about. We were like the guy in that movie. We wanted to get into show business. We were fascinated by celebrities. Now we're part of it. It's very strange."

De Niro had been the first of the two men to take a shine to Rupert. In the early 1970s, the actor had been given the script by its author, Paul D. Zimmerman, a *Newsweek* film critic who wanted to write about the country's growing obsession with celebrity culture. Zimmerman once recalled, "Bobby understood the bravery of Rupert Pupkin, his chutzpah, the simplicity of his motives. Bobby said he liked the single-minded sense of purpose. People speak of Bobby as an instinctive actor but he also understands these characters on an intellectual level.

I think Bobby understood Rupert because he's an obsessive person himself."

Scorsese wasn't as quick to sign up for the script, which was originally titled *Harry, the King of Comedy*. De Niro sent him the screenplay around the time the director was working on *Alice Doesn't Live Here Anymore*. Scorsese responded to the writing and thought the script was "hilarious," but he worried that it "was just a one-line gag: you won't let me go on the show, so I'll kidnap you and you'll put me on the show."

Interestingly, when *The King of Comedy* hit U.S. theaters in 1983, that barebones plot remained intact: Rupert, with the assistance of his equally whacked-out friend Masha (Sandra Bernhard), takes Jerry Langford (Jerry Lewis) hostage.

Despite his initial reluctance, Scorsese found himself connecting with Zimmerman's story in a deeper way over time. "It was between '75 to 1980 before I could actually get [the script]," Scorsese

BELOW: Jerry Lewis, Martin Scorsese, and Robert De Niro confer on the set of *The King of Comedy*.

said at a 2013 screening of *The King of Comedy*. "I discovered it as I went along." In a press release that announced this 30th anniversary digitally restored screening, he elaborated, saying, "I've always been partial to comedians—the irreverence, the absurdity, the hostility, all the feelings under the surface—and to the old world of late night variety shows hosted by Steve Allen and Jack Paar and, of course, Johnny Carson, to the familiarity and the camaraderie between the guests. You had the feeling that they were there with you, in your living room. Robert De Niro and I were both drawn to Paul Zimmerman's script for *The King of Comedy*, which really captured the show business atmosphere and the desperate attachments that some of the people on the other side of the screen could form, the ones that in certain cases turned dangerous."

THE PERFORMANCE

"I liked the character and I thought it was funny," De Niro once said of Rupert Pupkin. "We shot it on the streets of New York City and it gave us the opportunity to use things that we both knew happened there... One time an old lady, just a regular person, came over. I was sitting down outside of the building waiting for Jerry to come out. She came over and started talking to me and she kissed me and said something to me. It was very cute and funny and everyone laughed. We'd use spontaneous things like that."

That spontaneity gave *The King of Comedy* its vital, only-in-New-York unpredictability, a specialty of Scorsese's. But the film also extended his career-long fascination with loners while also viewing them with a fresh mixture of sympathy and fear. Rupert Pupkin had elements of Travis Bickle and Jake LaMotta—understandable, considering that they're all played by the same actor—but those men had been compelling physical presences. Rupert, by contrast, is pathetic, his mediocrity oozing from every pore.

To achieve the effect, De Niro studied stand-ups on the road. But he also got an insight into Rupert's personality when he was searching for the character's wardrobe. "We went to this store on Broadway, Blue Mountain," De Niro said in 2013. "We saw [Rupert's red suit] on a mannequin and said, 'Let's just do that.'" Scorsese added, "The face, mustache, and shirt were all there. The red tie and everything. We said, 'That's him, let's do it.'"

"Bobby's performance ... allowed him to drop a lot of the macho, tough-guy posturing that he had to do to elevate those other characters," Bernhard would later say. "I think he allowed himself to be a geek, and that's not easy for a guy like De Niro."

But that didn't make the actor any less imposing on the set. Jerry Lewis would later note that De Niro had not wanted to be friends with him during the shoot because, according to De Niro, "I really want to kill you in this picture... I wanna blow your head off, so how can we have dinner?"

TOP LEFT: Jerry Lewis and Robert De Niro.

BOTTOM LEFT: Rupert, desperately waiting for a callback from his hero, Jerry Langford.

III. THE PRODUCTION DESIGN

The King of Comedy's production designer was Boris Leven. A nine-time Oscar nominee—he won for his work on *West Side Story* with Victor A. Gangelin—Leven had worked on *Giant*, *Anatomy of a Murder*, *The Sound of Music*, and *The Andromeda Strain* before he first started collaborating with Scorsese on *New York, New York*. "Since the old Hollywood sets didn't exist anymore, I had Boris Leven … build them," Scorsese said of his homage to bygone Hollywood musicals. "In the city streets I'd seen in MGM and Warner Bros. musicals, New York curbs were always shown as very high and clean. When I was a child, I realized that wasn't right but was part of a whole mythical city that they had created. Now I wanted to re-create that mythical city…"

Leven's production design often emphasized an enhanced realism: just like the real thing, except slightly more intense, more vivid. He died in 1986 at the age of 78, just shortly before the release of the last film he designed for Scorsese, *The Color of Money*. Of his legacy, Leven once said, "In my work I have always tried to achieve the greatest simplicity, both in form and style, and in my life and relationship with other human beings, I have tried to be as honest with them as I am with myself."

The man's process was on great display in *The King of Comedy*'s signature scene (above). Excited about his chance to submit his work to Jerry Langford, Rupert prepares a reel of his stand-up routine. The scene starts innocently enough: Rupert sits at a desk in his parents' basement, recording a greeting to Jerry that will set up the comedy routine. (Sadly, his confident patter keeps getting interrupted by the annoyed off-screen protestations of his mother, played by Scorsese's own mom, Catherine, who had a cameo in a handful of his movies.) But then, Rupert tells Jerry how he should be introduced—"Will you please give your warmest welcome to the newest king of comedy, Rupert Pupkin!"—and the scene cuts to a black-and-white image of a cheering, laughing crowd. We hear applause and then we see Rupert's back as he addresses this fake audience. Intriguingly, Scorsese lets us hear very little of Rupert's routine, as the applause and laughter, ghostly and sterile, drowns out his words. At the same time, the camera slowly pulls back, revealing the immensity of the photo, the antiseptic silver walls and ceiling, and what looks like a parquet floor.

The image should be heroic—Rupert killing it as a stand-up—but everything about the scene is distorted.

The crowd isn't there. Rupert gets smaller and smaller in the frame. And, unlike the rest of the film's mostly realistic tone, this scene appears to be occurring in some nether world, presumably in Rupert's sick mind. And Leven's production design honors that approach, bringing a sense of off-kilter reality to a scene that's more upsetting the more we think about it. In Rupert's delusion, the audience is always there, obediently worshipping his every word, even when he's just telling them that he grew up in New Jersey.

ABOVE: In a simple but effective move, the camera rolls slowly back to reveal the giant photograph on the wall and Rupert Pupkin's strange, empty surroundings.

IV. KEEPING IT REAL

"I made a clear decision when I decided to make the picture to create no difference between the fantasies and reality," Martin Scorsese told film critic Richard Schickel. "Because if things are going on in your mind, and you can't go to sleep, and you're going over discussions and arguments, it's real. It's really happening… The fantasy is real."

Scorsese is correct in regards to most of *The King of Comedy*. Earlier in the story when Rupert fantasizes about Jerry begging him to take over the show for six weeks, it's shot and edited as realistically (and intentionally banally) as everything else in the movie.

But the imaginary stand-up scene is the one jarring exception—intentionally so. It provides the most unfiltered glimpse into Rupert's psyche, presented quickly and starkly about 30 minutes into the film so that its uncomfortable memory lingers in the viewer's mind for the rest of its running time.

The brief scene is also a teasing hint of what's to come when Rupert, against all odds, manages to appear on the *Jerry Langford Show* at the end of *The King of Comedy*, delivering that same stand-up material. And once we hear it, the routine surprises us in ways both good and bad. For one thing, it's actually funnier than perhaps we expected. But it's also darker, Rupert throwing autobiographical comments about an abusive father, alcoholic mother, and an unhappy life at school into the mix as "jokes" that don't land. The scene earlier on was Rupert's "idealized" impression of his stand-up career—that it stands in such sharp contrast to reality makes it all the more tragic and despairing.

BELOW: "Better to be king for a night than schmuck for a lifetime"—Rupert finally makes it onto the *Jerry Langford Show*.

A LOOMING STRIKE

Simplicity and honesty are the cornerstones of *The King of Comedy*'s visual style. In part, this was due to necessity. While the film was in the midst of preproduction, the possibility of a Directors Guild of America strike threatened the shooting schedule. As Scorsese explained later, "If you didn't start shooting by a certain date and have four weeks of important scenes—not just a character crossing the street—in the can, then the film would be stopped while you were shooting." Consequently, Scorsese had to begin production about a month before he was ready. Additionally, the director wasn't feeling well, and the accelerated shooting schedule only exacerbated his illness. "I shouldn't have done it and it soon became clear that I wasn't up to it," he confessed. "By the second week of shooting I was begging them not to let me go on. I was coughing on the floor and sounding like a character from *The Magic Mountain*!"

A STRAIGHTFORWARD VISUAL PALETTE

Scorsese had wanted to keep *The King of Comedy*'s visual palette straightforward, resisting the operatic flourish he'd brought to *Raging Bull*. He explained his thought process in *Scorsese on Scorsese*: "People had reacted in such a way to *Raging Bull*, saying it was a beautiful film—like *Days of Heaven*, you could take every frame and put it on the wall—that I decided my next picture was going to be 1903 style, more like Edwin S. Porter's *Life of an American Fireman* (below), with no close-ups. So in *King of Comedy* that's what I tried to do."

BELOW: Scene stills from *Life of an American Fireman*, a six-minute short released in 1903 and one of the first narrative films.

V. THE FILM'S LEGACY

For a film about showbiz success, *The King of Comedy*, ironically, didn't find much of its own. Only earning about $2.5 million, the film grossed far less than Scorsese's previous features. Years later, the director could still remember watching an *Entertainment Tonight* broadcast on New Year's Eve that offered a look back at 1983's film highlights. As he was preparing to go out for the evening, the show declared, "And now for the flop of the year: *The King of Comedy*!"

In a sense, *The King of Comedy*'s commercial failure was understandable: a movie about a strange little nobody like Rupert Pupkin was probably never destined to catch on with the public. Scorsese had been drawn to *The King of Comedy* because he recognized himself in both Rupert and Jerry Langford: the needy up-and-comer and the

established artist who had to be mindful of the ravenous masses. (Don't forget that John W. Hinckley, Jr., the assassin who tried to kill President Ronald Reagan in 1981, had been a fan of Scorsese's *Taxi Driver*, plotting the murder as a way to attract the attention of co-star Jodie Foster.) But in a cruel twist of fate, the film's box-office struggles cut short Scorsese's comeback after *Raging Bull*, sending him into a period of soul-searching and change-of-pace creative choices. Making a movie about the struggle to be discovered resulted in its maker having to begin a process of being rediscovered.

Still, he was in good company. As he recalled in *Robert Altman: The Oral Biography*, Scorsese ran into the maverick filmmaker in '83 when they were both at a low point commercially. "[W]hen it opened in 1983, *The King of Comedy* was considered a terrible

ABOVE: Jerry Lewis and Robert De Niro share a laugh on set. Though a commercial bust, *The King of Comedy* did win a BAFTA award for its screenplay, the National Society of Film Critics prize for Sandra Bernhard for Best Supporting Actress, and Film of the year from the London Critics Circle.

flop," Scorsese said. "[Altman's 1980 film] *HealtH* was hardly opened. I happened to mention to him that *King of Comedy* was pretty much dropped from distribution by Fox, and I mentioned the name of the man who did it. And he said, 'That's exactly the same person who dropped *HealtH*.' In a way, he was sent to the diaspora for ten years, and so was I."

The film remains one of Scorsese's prickliest, a darkly funny and yet sobering snapshot of life in the media age. *The King of Comedy* isn't easy to watch, even for Scorsese. In *Conversations With Scorsese*, the filmmaker admits that he identified with Rupert's fascination with stardom. "When I first went to L.A. in 1970, there was a little bit of that need in me—to buy into, participate in, the dream world of celebrity," he said. "It's almost as if they are like gods and goddesses—that's the impression [stars] make on you from when you're four or five years old."

Asked for his impressions of the film more than 25 years after its release, Scorsese confessed, "I haven't seen it since I made it. It's too embarrassing."

"As I was making the film," he said, "I realized that a part of me was in that story, and I was forced to confront it. I look back now and I realize why I couldn't make *King of Comedy* back in 1975 when De Niro first gave it to me. I was too close to it. I didn't understand it."

SUMMARY OF TECHNIQUE

1. MIXING REALITY AND FANTASY
Much of *The King of Comedy* is played straight, even when we're inside Rupert's delusions. This sequence, however, is striking because it's a perversion of reality. As a result, it's even more upsetting by contrast.

2. SOUND DESIGN
By playing with what we hear—muffling Rupert's stand-up act and introducing oddly unsettling laughter—Scorsese creates a distorted hall-of-mirrors reality. All of the sounds are naturalistic, but by tweaking them, they suddenly feel surreal, alien. It's a perfect sonic equivalent to the twisted fantasies bouncing around in Rupert's head.

3. MOVING CAMERA
Slowly tracking back from Rupert, whose back is to us, Scorsese minimizes the moment of Rupert's imagined triumph. Rather than growing larger in the frame, the character shrinks, the filmmaker's subtle way of suggesting that what we're seeing is a fantasy that won't ever come to light.

4. STERILE PRODUCTION DESIGN
Production designer Boris Leven utilizes two important pieces of décor to emphasize the scene's strangeness. The first is the sterile, cold walls around Rupert, which robs the moment of any warmth or excitement. The second is the shockingly large black-and-white photo of the audience clapping and laughing. Frozen on the wall, this crowd is stripped of its humanity, suggesting that Rupert's imagined adoring throngs are nothing but a futile illusion.

GOODFELLAS
1990

SCREENPLAY:
Nicholas Pileggi and Martin Scorsese (Based on the book *Wiseguy* by Nicholas Pileggi)

CINEMATOGRAPHER:
Michael Ballhaus

EDITOR:
Thelma Schoonmaker

PRODUCTION DESIGNER:
Kristi Zea

PRINCIPAL SCENE ACTORS:
Ray Liotta (Henry Hill)
Lorraine Bracco (Karen Hill)
Henny Youngman (Henny Youngman)

SCENE:
The Copacabana sequence

06

I. INTRODUCTION

Characters in Martin Scorsese's movies often have big dreams. In *The Aviator*, Howard Hughes wants notoriety as a Hollywood kingmaker and aviation guru. In *The King of Comedy*, Rupert Pupkin wants to be a famous stand-up comedian. In the drama *Goodfellas*, Henry Hill makes his aspirations clear from the outset: "As far back as I can remember," he tells us through voiceover, "I always wanted to be a gangster."

A meditation on the seductive allure of evil, *Goodfellas* is one of the filmmaker's most enduring works. Scorsese had made movies about mobsters—he grew up observing the lifestyle in his New York neighborhood—but this story about real-life hood Henry Hill gave him a chance to articulate what draws so many people to a life of crime. For some, it's about power. For others, it's about having opportunities not afforded in the conventional world. Both of these factors appealed to Hill, but *Goodfellas* suggests there was something else about the gangster milieu that hooked him: He wanted to feel special. He wanted to be somebody.

The Oscar-nominated film's most iconic scene remains a powerhouse both technically and thematically. Illustrating the longings of its charming antihero, played by Ray Liotta, the sequence (commonly known as the "Copacabana sequence") takes Hill and his girlfriend Karen from a busy city street all the way to the front row of an exclusive nightspot. With one unbroken tracking shot, Scorsese and his crew illustrate the breadth of Hill's influence, seducing both Karen and the audience in the process. All at once, we understand why Hill wanted to be a gangster—and, later, why his downfall will be so agonizing for him.

RIGHT: Henry Hill (Ray Liotta), at far right, is drawn into the mob life.

II. SETTING THE SCENE

In the book *Wiseguy*, crime writer Nicholas Pileggi documented the exploits of real-life gangster Henry Hill. When Scorsese decided to turn the book into a film, there was only a brief mention of Hill's nights at the Copacabana. "On crowded nights, when people were lined up outside and couldn't get in," Pileggi wrote in the book, "the doormen used to let Henry and our party in through the kitchen, which was filled with Chinese cooks, and we'd go upstairs and sit down immediately."

"A couple of lines in a book in the hands of the director, that's where you begin to see a nonfiction book in detail really blossom into a kind of art," said Pileggi, who co-wrote the screenplay with Scorsese.

"The whole idea is that it had to be done in one take so you don't feel like it was a series of cuts or that there was a separation between [Henry] and the world that he was trying to get into," Scorsese would later say about his instinct for shooting the scene. "The camera flowed … and just glided through this world—just all the doors opened to him and everything just slipped away. It was like heaven. And then to emerge [in front of the stage], the king and queen, this was the highest he could aspire to."

The film's production designer, two-time Oscar-nominee Kristi Zea, recognized that the sequence was key in Henry and Karen's early relationship. "This was the mating dance," she later said. "Henry's arrival into the Copa, the way he came in, and how

the whole thing was designed to impress the hell out of Karen. You wanted the audience to be part of her being impressed."

But although Scorsese's strategy was driven by the dramatic and emotional impact he wanted to produce, there may have been other factors at play as well. Actress Illeana Douglas, who played Rosie in the film and was dating Scorsese at the time, once observed, "Brian De Palma had just done this incredibly long Steadicam® shot in *The Untouchables*, and Marty said it would be funny to try to do it one minute longer than De Palma's. The world perceives this as 'Oh, the Copacabana scene!' But what it really is, is directors behind the scenes having fun fucking with each other."

LEFT & ABOVE: Ray Liotta plays Henry Hill, a young man determined to make it as a gangster, who is taken under the wing of Paul "Paulie" Cicero (Paul Sorvino, at left with Liotta), James "Jimmy the Gent" Conway (Robert De Niro), and Tommy DeVito (Joe Pesci, above with De Niro and Liotta).

THE WISEGUY

When Martin Scorsese was working on *The Color of Money*, he saw a glowing review in the *New York Review of Books* for *Wiseguy*, an account of the life of mobster Henry Hill who had become an FBI informant. Although Scorsese had already made movies about gangsters, *Wiseguy* piqued his interest because the book "was telling the story in a different way. It's about that lifestyle, and the dangerous seduction of that lifestyle."

According to Nicholas Pileggi, the crime reporter who wrote *Wiseguy* and co-authored the *Goodfellas* screenplay with Scorsese, Hill "was a middle-level hustler… His job was to hustle money. He was what they call an earner. He was hyperactive. According to his mother, he never stopped. He would run through the house, slam doors." Scorsese found Hill fascinating. "He was upset but not sorry for the things he had done. At the end, he regrets that he's no longer a wiseguy, but there's no hypocrisy about being sorry for his life, it's just 'Gee, no more fun.' …I think the audience should get angry at him and I would hope they do—and maybe with the system which allows this."

Scorsese cast character actor Ray Liotta (below) for the role—an unpopular choice with the studio, which wanted a star for the lead. Said Liotta years later, "They would have rather had Eddie Murphy than me."

ABOVE: Former American mobster, Henry Hill.

III. THE LONG TAKE

There have been several famous unbroken tracking shots across film history—the openings of *Touch of Evil* and *The Player*, the chaotic car chase in *Children of Men*—but few have been so important in establishing character as the famous Copacabana sequence in *Goodfellas*. It's not simply bravura filmmaking, it plunges us directly into the excitement and status that the movie's central character, Henry Hill, has craved since childhood. For a few moments, we are wrapped up in the same giddy luxuriance that has entranced our main character.

By this point in *Goodfellas*, Henry, a Brooklyn kid longing to be a part of the gangster lifestyle he saw while growing up in his neighborhood, has already begun to work his way up the ladder of the organization, winning the trust of senior lieutenants Jimmy Conway (Robert De Niro) and Tommy DeVito (Joe Pesci).

But the Copacabana sequence, set in the late 1960s, doesn't feature any of Henry's associates—it instead focuses on the woman he's trying to woo. Karen (Lorraine Bracco) is smitten by this brash, charming young man, but before he takes her to the Copa, she still doesn't know much about him. The scene allows Henry to demonstrate to her precisely where he stands in the local pecking order.

Filmed with a Steadicam—which permits a smooth, effortless glide through space—the Copacabana sequence starts out on the street as Henry and Karen exit his car and proceed to the club. Karen can't believe he can simply leave his car with an attendant, but the surprises are just beginning. With utter nonchalance, Henry leads her to a side entrance into the busy club, moving through the kitchen and right to the front of the stage, warmly greeted by everyone he meets. Bewildered and more than a little impressed, she asks him what he does. "I'm in construction," he lies. She doesn't respond, but her face suggests that she's not quite sure she believes him—or that she necessarily minds.

ABOVE: Garrett Brown with his Steadicam, 1976.

The sequence is a superb combination of technical craftsmanship and nuanced performances. Liotta is all smooth confidence, but Bracco's enigmatic turn suggests her character's complicity in her soon-to-be-husband's crimes. Karen knows he doesn't work in construction, and she probably knows how he actually makes his living. But after having the door to a better life opened to her, she chooses to keep her mouth shut, to look the other way and enjoy the evening. And that's the secret allure of *Goodfellas* in a nutshell: Scorsese asks us to identify with the trappings of success through illicit means, illustrating how easy it is to be enchanted by the criminal lifestyle.

THE STEADICAM

The Copacabana sequence was filmed with a Steadicam, a device that allows a camera operator to move through space freely without upsetting the camera. As a result, a director can produce smooth, balletic, gliding shots. The Steadicam was created in the mid-1970s by Garrett Brown, a camera operator who has gone on to use his invention memorably in films like *The Shining* and Martin Scorsese's *Casino*.

"A good Steadicam shot is the combination of an artistic idea and a good story, but also there's this dance component," Brown has said. "It is so incredibly much fun to shoot Steadicam, because you have the artistic bit, you have the continuity of a move that does something, that has an emotional whack to it. And then you have the dancer's tasks of navigating and not falling down, and the more gracefully you can do it, the better the shot looks."

IV. THE LOGISTICS

What would come to be *Goodfellas'* signature scene didn't start off as such. In fact, certain crewmembers had their doubts. Larry McConkey, a Steadicam operator who has worked with Spike Lee, the Coen brothers, and Brian De Palma, admitted, "The impression I had when Marty walked us through the Copacabana shot was that this is going to be the most boring, worst thing I've ever done. We're walking across the street, down the stairs, down a hallway, in the kitchen... What is this shot about?"

"I never even knew when we were making it what that scene was," actress Lorraine Bracco said in 2004. "I never knew—I was clueless. I had never even seen a Steadicam."

Obviously, such a complicated shot would prove challenging to put together. "There were 400 or more absolutely precise timing moments," McConkey said. "It was totally impossible, mathematically."

Also adding to the difficulty was that Scorsese's idea for the choreography of the scene didn't mesh with the logistics of the locations. "He wanted a long preamble before they get into the [nightclub]," recalled Zea. "The Copa didn't have a long enough walk before they actually get into the nightclub. So we had to build a hallway, and we literally took the walls away while the camera was in motion, so that they were gone by the time Ray and Lorraine showed up in the main room. The delivery of the camera into that big space had to be done like a ballet. Henry is saying hi to everyone, everyone knew who he was. And then the table flies across the camera and lands smack dab in front of [comic] Henny Youngman, and suddenly there's champagne coming over courtesy of these other guys."

"It was kind of tricky to get all the actions right because Marty is so very accurate about every single timing," cinematographer Michael Ballhaus said. "You know, what the people do in the kitchen, the guy with the table comes at the right time and brings the table over. All these things were very important."

The specificity wasn't simply the whims of an exacting director. *Goodfellas* is in part Scorsese's reflection of his own youth as an impressionable, asthmatic voyeur observing the colorful characters around him. As McConkey recalled, "Marty watches the first rehearsal, and the only thing he said was,

ABOVE: "When the table comes in, it's got to fly in!" Steadicam operator Larry McConkey remembered Scorsese saying.

'No, no! When the table comes in, it's got to fly in! I came here as a kid and I saw this!'"

THE CINEMATOGRAPHER

Cinematographer Michael Ballhaus started his collaboration with Martin Scorsese in the mid-'80s on *After Hours*. But he had been a fan of the filmmaker's ever since seeing *Taxi Driver* and *Boxcar Bertha*. "I saw Marty once from afar, when he came to [the] Berlin [Film Festival] for the screening of *Raging Bull*," Ballhaus said. "I still remember how I sat at the Zoo-Palast and blurted out to [my wife], 'One day I must make a film with this man.'"

By the time they worked on *Goodfellas*, they had already made three films together. "Marty is the only director for whom I will do anything," Ballhaus once said. "And of course, a Mafia tale like *Goodfellas*—with so much brutality, dead bodies, murders, and a very dark storyline—was hardly my favorite genre. But as we all know now, the brilliant aspect of this film is that it shows the other side of the Mafia: not only its glorified atmosphere, but also the dirty side of the business."

Still, the film's level of violence affected Ballhaus. "You end up discussing whether the murder victim on the bed had enough brains splattered around him, or whether blood that was sprayed on bed sheets should really be darker," he recalled. "It isn't funny when one speaks of death as if it were a matter of having more or less salt in your soup."

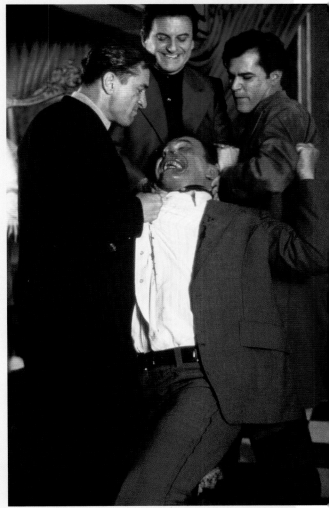

BELOW: Martin Scorsese with cinematographer Michael Ballhaus.

RIGHT & ABOVE RIGHT: Though Ballhaus was affected by the level of violence in *Goodfellas*, he trusted Scorsese, for whom he would "do anything."

ABOVE: "Henny Youngman came on stage and forgot his lines!"

V. FILMING THE SCENE

"It's probably the hardest orchestrated single shot I've ever been involved in," said Scorsese's longtime first assistant director Joseph Reidy.

The scene was filmed seven or eight times and, according to Ballhaus, took less than a full day to shoot. Part of the relative ease of executing the scene was that Ballhaus had already worked with Scorsese on a few films, including *The Last Temptation of Christ* and *After Hours*. The two men had established an excellent working relationship. "Scorsese gives me a shot list four weeks before we start shooting," Ballhaus explained. "That means that various parameters are noted along the margins of the script … As soon as he hands me his wish list, everything is in my hands. The beautiful thing is that the images I realize match his concepts and imagination."

One of the interesting adventures in filming the scene—not to mention the entire movie—was finding background actors for the complicated shot. Johnny Ciarcia, who had a bit part in *Goodfellas*, told *GQ*, "Marty Scorsese was in trouble for extras, so one of the casting directors called me. I live on Mulberry Street. I know the whole world. I went and I made a deal for $10 a person. We had five busloads of people on Fifth Avenue for the Copa. I set it all up." As to who these people were specifically, Douglas says, "Let's say we had a lot of set visits … from certain people. There were a lot of people in the film where it was, nudge-nudge, wink-wink, 'Make sure she gets on camera, otherwise Local 19 is going to be a little upset with us.' There was a great sense of blurring the lines."

Or, as co-star Debi Mazar put it, "The short answer is yes, a lot of the extras were gangsters."

The intense choreography of the scene also imposed certain technical obstacles for Ballhaus. "[W]e had to build the rear entrance to the kitchen of the original club on location," he said. "I was thinking mainly about how we could go in from the outside. The task was hard enough and I didn't want to pull the aperture as well. In those days, we didn't have a remote control for the Steadicam, with which one could have adjusted the aperture."

And yet, the Copa sequence is a graceful, exhilarating set piece in the movie, even if its makers still recall that its finale, involving veteran comic Henny Youngman delivering his famous "Take my wife, please!" line, proved trickier than expected. "After we had about four minutes perfectly in the can," Ballhaus noted, "Henny Youngman came on stage and forgot his lines! … He forgot his line that he had said about 2,000 times!"

VI. THE LEGACY

The Copa sequence was quickly hailed as a landmark, the icing on the cake being the use of the Crystals' romantic R&B hit "Then He Kissed Me" on top of the sequence. "He's one of the few people who knows how to match music and picture," director Spike Lee has said about Scorsese. "It's not just about taking a great record and just slapping it up in there."

Goodfellas has become one of Scorsese's preeminent films, with an Oscar won for Joe Pesci's supporting performance, but it has also been hugely influential. For one thing, its regular-joe portrayal of the East Coast mob helped pave the way for the acclaimed TV drama The Sopranos. (Actor Michael Imperioli, who was part of Goodfellas and The Sopranos, told GQ, "Probably 80 percent of the cast ended up on The Sopranos.")

But the film's bravura style, as demonstrated by the Copa sequence, inspired filmmaker Paul Thomas Anderson's Boogie Nights—particularly the latter's grandiose opening shot that starts out on the street before swooping into a disco club.

"He threw the cinematic fucking sink into that movie," Anderson said of Goodfellas. "Some stuff I did in Boogie Nights is compared to the long traveling shot into the Copacabana. But there have been so many shots like it... What's obnoxious and so fucking brilliant about Scorsese is that he does these pretentious, insane camera moves that suddenly make sense. He's the biggest show-off—and we don't even see it."

For Scorsese's part, the Copa sequence was about trying to put the audience into the mindset of the aspiring, materialistic Henry before laying bare the consequences of such an immoral life. "When you were able to get a table [at the Copa], it was like being in the court of the kings," he once said. "The mob guys were really the ones in charge. The Copa lounge was always more significant because the real guys were up there... Everyone paid for the privilege eventually. The danger of [Goodfellas] is that young people could look at it and think, 'Hey, what a great life.' But you've got to see the last hour of the picture when things start going wrong in a big way."

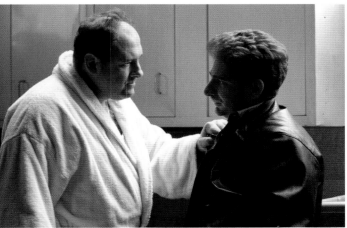

SUMMARY OF TECHNIQUE

1. USE OF STEADICAM
The camera gives a sense of movement through space, which creates a feeling of energy and freedom in the scene. Instead of seeming static, the Copa sequence has the spontaneity and unpredictability of life, which leaves the viewer off-balance and intrigued. We're as shocked and delighted as Karen as Henry leads her through the hallways and kitchen out into the club.

2. A SINGLE SHOT
By not cutting, Scorsese creates a headlong rush that's uninterrupted. Through the use of a gliding camera, the filmmaker captures the euphoria and anxiety of a first date, externalizing the emotions the budding lovers are feeling.

3. SHOWING RATHER THAN TELLING
A lesser film would have demonstrated Henry Hill's power and influence through dialogue. But in the Copa sequence, *Goodfellas* illustrates it visually, showing us that Henry has privileges and respect that others don't enjoy. He can enter the club through a door that no one else is allowed to use. Everyone in the kitchen loves him. He gets his own special table near the stage. The entire shot is constructed to emphasize Henry's elevated status with a minimum of dialogue.

4. SHOWMANSHIP
Though the sequence is undoubtedly bravura, it's at the service of character and theme. The filmmaking is flawless and innovative, seeking to seduce the audience in the same way that Karen is wowed by Henry's impressive connections and implied status.

TOP: Martin Scorsese and Oscar winner Joe Pesci on set.

OPPOSITE MIDDLE: Spike Lee taking a break during the filming of his 1989 drama, *Do the Right Thing*.

OPPOSITE BOTTOM: On the set of *Boogie Nights*, Paul Thomas Anderson directs Heather Graham.

ABOVE: James Gandolfini with Michael Imperioli in *The Sopranos*.

THE AGE OF INNOCENCE
1993

SCREENPLAY:
Jay Cocks and Martin Scorsese (Based upon
the novel by Edith Wharton)

CINEMATOGRAPHER:
Michael Ballhaus

EDITOR:
Thelma Schoonmaker

PRODUCTION DESIGNER:
Dante Ferretti

PRINCIPAL SCENE ACTORS:
Daniel Day-Lewis (Newland Archer)
Michelle Pfeiffer (Ellen Olenska)
Robert Sean Leonard (Ted Archer)

SCENE:
Newland Archer walks away

07

I. INTRODUCTION

When Martin Scorsese's adaptation of Edith Wharton's novel, *The Age of Innocence,* opened in the fall of 1993, some people expressed confusion as to why a filmmaker so associated with violent themes would be drawn to a seemingly genteel romantic drama set in the 1870s, even if it did take place in New York City. But a comment Scorsese made years later explained the connection between *The Age of Innocence* and his other works: "I'm always interested in people who lose their world," he said in 2010.

Travis Bickle, Jake LaMotta, Henry Hill: They're all men shaped by their environment—and when it comes crashing down, they fall apart as well. But such a downfall has never been portrayed in a Scorsese picture as poignantly as it is in *The Age of Innocence.* The man in question is Newland Archer (Daniel Day-Lewis), a young, aristocratic lawyer engaged to the naïve but sweet-hearted May Welland (Winona Ryder). Their pairing will unite two prestigious New York families, but Archer finds himself attracted to the mysterious Ellen Olenska (Michelle Pfeiffer), a free spirit who is fleeing an unhappy marriage with a Polish count. Though there's a palpable attraction between Archer and Olenska, they cannot act upon it lest they become ostracized from their tight-knit community ruled by wealth and manners.

The doomed love story of *The Age of Innocence* reaches its apex in its final scene, which takes place decades after the film's central narrative. Now in his fifties, Archer has not seen Olenska for many years, instead choosing to stay with May and raise a family with her. Despite May's untimely death, he has remained faithful to their marriage vows, only finally being given a chance to see his true love when his adult son, Ted (Robert Sean Leonard), takes him on a trip to Paris, where he will meet up with the countess. But at the last moment, Archer resists visiting her apartment, instead letting his son say hello as he walks away.

An ambiguous ending—why would he not want to see her one last time?—is rendered powerfully, its intimations more tragic and emotional because of what is understood rather than for anything that is said in the moment. Scorsese's films are filled with violence, but they are also filled with longing, with hoped-for resolutions that don't come to pass.

The Age of Innocence is shattering without spilling an ounce of blood.

ABOVE: Michelle Pfeiffer as Ellen Olenska on the left, and
Winona Ryder on the right as May Welland, the woman
to whom Newland Archer is engaged.

II. FROM PAGE TO SCREEN

ABOVE: Michelle Pfeiffer and Daniel Day-Lewis in *The Age of Innocence*.

As is often the case with Scorsese's movies, *The Age of Innocence* was a project that someone close to the director recommended to him, only to be rebuffed until, years later, Scorsese found himself in the right frame of mind to make the film.

Jay Cocks, a onetime film critic for *Time*, became friends with Scorsese in the late 1960s. Sometime toward the beginning of the '80s, he suggested that Scorsese read Wharton's novel, which had won the Pulitzer Prize in 1921. The book provided a snapshot of upper-class New York in the 1870s, when strict social customs determined one's standing. In the midst of this stifling environment, a lawyer and a married countess—a cousin of his betrothed—begin to develop feelings for one another. The lawyer is too rigid to leave behind his life and run away with this woman, who wants to divorce her husband for his

cruel treatment of her. Instead, determined to do the "right" thing, the man tries to sweep his emotions under the rug, never quite succeeding.

As Cocks would recall years later, "On some mysterious impulse that I still don't quite understand, I said to Marty one night when we were having dinner, 'You oughta read this book, it'll make a wonderful movie—the kind of movie that we love but hasn't really been done too much these days. It's a love story.'"

"He tried to sell me on it, telling me a little about the story," Scorsese once remarked, "but I wasn't interested. I was finishing up *Raging Bull*, and was about to go into *The King of Comedy*, and the moods of those films were eating into my lifestyle, which was not conducive to thinking about this novel. I eventually read the book in 1987; by then a number

COLD-BLOODED MANNERS

The deceptive refinement of Wharton's novel—mixed with the fact that any faithful adaptation would be classified as a "costume drama"—seems at odds with Scorsese's visceral, brutal, vulgar oeuvre. But Scorsese hooked into Wharton's depiction of a New York where oppressive social codes must be obeyed. For a man born roughly 70 years after the events depicted in the book, the milieu didn't seem that alien.

"What has always stuck in my head is the brutality under the manners," he said in 1993. "People hide what they mean under the surface of language. In the subculture I was around when I grew up in Little Italy, when somebody was killed, there was a finality to it. It was usually done by the hands of a friend. And in a funny way, it was almost like ritualistic slaughter, a sacrifice. But New York society in the 1870s didn't have that. It was so cold-blooded. I don't know which is preferable. I grew up thinking in one way, but in my own private life the past ten years, I've started to appreciate the ability to say a little in certain emotional situations and mean a lot."

As is often the case in Scorsese's films, the devil is in the detail—the visual subtext (a camera pans back to linger on a painting of a woman being scalped, for example), and in snippets of action that speak to the cruelty and violence buried beneath the surface of manners and propriety.

ABOVE: The barely contained passion of *The Age of Innocence*, contrasted with the violence and aggression of previous Scorsese pictures: *The Last Temptation of Christ* (top left), *Cape Fear* (top right), *Goodfellas* (above).

of things in my life had calmed down and I was able to be a little more reflective."

The two men wrote the screenplay, with Scorsese taking particular interest in the thwarted love affair between the lawyer and the countess. Speaking with film critic Roger Ebert around the time of the film's release, Scorsese noted that Cocks had told him back in 1980, "'When you do your costume piece, when you do your romance, this is you.' Not meaning, of course, that I'm Archer or Ellen. It was the spirit

of it—the spirit of the exquisite romantic pain. The idea that the mere touching of a woman's hand would suffice. The idea that seeing her across the room would keep him alive for another year. That's something I guess that is part of me. He knew me, by that time, fairly well."

ABOVE: Ryan O'Neal and Marisa Berenson in *Barry Lyndon*.

III. INFLUENCES

ABOVE: *The Magnificent Ambersons* features the cavernous, uninviting rooms of the Amberson home.

Films from several different eras and nationalities informed the making of *The Age of Innocence*. The infrequent narration by Joanne Woodward, serving as a dispassionate observer and guide in *The Age of Innocence*, recalls a similar technique used brilliantly by Stanley Kubrick in his 1975 period picture, *Barry Lyndon*. Discussing Kubrick's film affectionately, Scorsese once noted that when he heard about the project he "hoped [Kubrick] was going to take the 'costume piece' somewhere else—and he took it back in time." Likewise, Scorsese was consciously influenced by the narration in *Barry Lyndon*, "how the narrator's voice helps get you to a certain contemplative state, almost like reading a novel from the nineteenth century. You hear the voice of Joanne Woodward, as Edith Wharton, right in your ear."

Another film with famous narration, *The Magnificent Ambersons*, also helped shape Scorsese's movie. Orson Welles' follow-up to *Citizen Kane* in 1942, adapted from Booth Tarkington's Pulitzer Prize-winning novel, was also a study in cultural morays, telling a tale of unrequited passions and a changing world as the industrial age takes hold.

"For Marty, *Ambersons* was a way into a world that he saw, heard about, experienced second- or third-hand through the movies," Jay Cocks once observed. And although Scorsese screened the film to prepare for *The Age of Innocence*, the director confessed that while he finds *Ambersons* "beautiful and moving ... I'm not a great devotee of it... I don't really understand the people, it's not a society I can easily relate to."

Tonally, *The Age of Innocence* drew inspiration from *The Heiress*, a 1949 romantic drama directed by William Wyler and starring Olivia de Havilland and Montgomery Clift. It was a movie that had transfixed Scorsese as a boy.

"One of the genres that I really admire is the costume piece, even the trashiest kind, like *The Count of Monte Cristo*," Scorsese said. "When I was nine or ten, my father took me to see *The Heiress*, which was the first costume piece that had a powerful impact on me. I didn't understand every detail, but I knew that something terrible had happened, a breach of trust and love—and everybody was dressed so nicely and they had such nice drawing rooms. I didn't understand how a father could talk that way to his daughter, explaining that the man was after her for her money,

'Because you're not clever and you're quite plain.' That's quite a scene."

The great Italian director Luchino Visconti's movies were also studied for *The Age of Innocence*, particularly his lush 1963 epic *The Leopard*. Dante Ferretti recalled that Scorsese screened the movie for his crew, giving his production designer specific instructions: "He said, 'If [you're] able to make 30 percent the film like Visconti did, I'm very happy.' I figure it did more than 30 percent—I think it did almost 110 percent."

"We tried to get the authenticity of Visconti, even though I couldn't hope to achieve the beauty of *The Leopard* or *Senso* or *The Innocent*," Scorsese said. "I loved those pictures, I watched them over and over."

BELOW: *The Heiress*, with Olivia de Havilland and Montgomery Clift. At top, William Wyler directs.

BELOW: The lush production of *The Leopard*, which was nominated for an Oscar for Best Costume Design, Color.

IV. WALKING AWAY

At the end of *The Age of Innocence*, it would appear that Newland Archer finally gets his wish. After years of being apart from the Countess Olenska, he arrives in Paris with his son Ted, learning that Ted is planning to visit her—and that Ted's mother, May, knew about Archer's unfulfilled love all along. But when Ted and Archer travel to Olenska's apartment, Archer demurs, staying in the courtyard while Ted goes up to greet her. The sunlight reflecting off her window reminds Archer of a crucial moment earlier in their lives, when he went to fetch her at the home of May's grandmother, Mrs. Mingott. But seeing the countess looking so lovely in the distance, Archer resisted going up to her—if he spoke to Olenska, he knew he wouldn't be able to be separated from her again. And so he walked away.

In the final moments of the film, Archer relives that earlier moment, which we see as a brief flashback. And then he once again walks away. Rather than going up to the countess's apartment, he stands up and leaves the courtyard without saying a word, his image getting smaller and smaller in the distance, until he disappears.

Since 1993 when *The Age of Innocence* debuted, audiences have been torn by the film's last, unresolved note. Speaking with critic Richard Schickel almost twenty years later, Scorsese noted, "Jay Cocks said … that people never forgave the fact that Daniel Day-Lewis and Michelle Pfeiffer don't get to make love in the film. But that's the story."

The scene was shot in Paris, and the filmmaker has remarked that while staging the sequence, cinematographer Michael Ballhaus pressed him to give the film a happier ending. "[He] goes, 'Oh, why can't he go upstairs? …At last, he could safely embrace Ellen.'" But Scorsese was insistent. "I said, 'He can't. He can't go up. That's what she loved about him. What are you going to do, be inconsistent at the last minute?'"

At the film's twentieth anniversary screening at the New York Film Festival, Scorsese was still discussing the movie's bittersweet tone and its unrequited ending. Describing the movie as evoking "memory, loss, sort of a melancholia," he said, "I keep thinking of Mr. Bernstein [played by Everett Sloane] in *Citizen Kane* where he says, 'There isn't one day that goes by where I haven't thought of that young woman I saw on the ferry forty years ago.' This is more explored than that, but that's the idea."

Often in Scorsese's movies, the male character doesn't end up with the woman of his dreams—or, if he does, the seeming angel turns into a nightmare, usually because of the man's failings. *The Age of Innocence* is the purest expression of the filmmaker's attraction to stories about love fading, or defeated by insurmountable obstacles. "What's very significant to me is that when you fall in love, you can't see what other people see," Scorsese once remarked. "You become as passionate and obsessive as Newland, who can't see what's going on around him. And I was also fascinated by the sense of loss in the love story. A situation where just a touch of the hand would suffice, not necessarily for the consummation of the relationship, but at least to keep him alive, and to keep each other alive for a few months. ... It seems to be a theme I like a lot, and it's in movies like *Who's That Knocking at My Door* or *Taxi Driver* ... I can identify with those feelings of wanting to take and not taking, of wanting to proceed with something and not proceeding, for many different reasons—shyness, a certain kind of propriety, or deciding that it wasn't such a great idea."

ABOVE: The ambiguous ending of *The Age of Innocence* has troubled viewers over the years, yet the lack of resolution or explanation is typical of Scorsese's approach. The filmmaker allows audiences to wonder at his characters' motives, appreciating that, in life, decisions are rarely simple.

V. A PERSONAL CONNECTION

To understand Scorsese's deep sympathy for Archer's dutiful behavior—this is a man who prized his family obligations over his own desires—one should remember that the movie is dedicated to the filmmaker's father, Charles Scorsese, who died shortly before *The Age of Innocence*'s premiere at the Venice Film Festival.

As Scorsese would later put it, "That was the last film of mine my father saw…When I was making the film, I was thinking very much about my father's sense of obligation and responsibility—what he did for us, whether he was massaging me with alcohol to get a fever down or going through all this madness with doctors, not having an education, not knowing how to deal with all this. I thought that Newland Archer, when he decides to stay [with May], is demonstrating that kind of responsibility."

Throughout his career, the opinion of his father has been important to Scorsese. At the screening of *Raging Bull* for United Artists, after a moment's tense silence, the head of the company, Andy Albeck, rose and shook Scorsese's hand, saying, "Mr. Scorsese, you are an artist." Reportedly, the praise itself meant less to Scorsese than the fact that his father overheard it. Charles Scorsese also shaped his son's ideas of New York, possibly influencing his decision to make *Gangs of New York*. Shortly after the film's release in 2003, Scorsese told the *Guardian*, "My father had this mythological sense of the old New York, and he used to tell me stories about these old gangs, particularly the Forty Thieves in the Fourth Ward."

Speaking at a twentieth-anniversary screening, Scorsese commented on Archer's decision and the way that it rankled some audiences. "It's unacceptable,

ABOVE: Scorsese with his father Charles and mother Catherine.

RIGHT: Scorsese behind the camera shooting *The Age of Innocence*.

I guess, in our world now," he said of the character's choice to remain loyal. "[Nowadays] if you have a chance at freedom, take it, go for it. Ultimately, when you get it, what do you do with it?"

Further elaborating on his mindset, Scorsese said in a separate interview, "Essentially, [Archer] is what they call in America a 'stand-up guy'—a man of principle who would not abandon his wife and children. When he really wanted something, he gave it up because of his child. That's very interesting to me. I don't know if I or a lot of other people could do the same, but I know that even today there are many who would. It's about making a decision in life and sticking to it, making do with what you have."

ABOVE: Initially, Daniel Day-Lewis was reluctant to take the part of Newland Archer. "Too English," the actor said of the role. "I was hoping he'd ask me to do something more rough-and-tumble."

LEFT: Elmer Bernstein worked with Martin Scorsese on three films: *Cape Fear*, *The Age of Innocence*, and *Bringing Out the Dead*.

VI. THE MUSIC

In a film where the characters can't express their emotions for fear of reprisals, the score can help disclose the lovers' buried feelings, giving voice to the anguish under the surface of their guarded expressions. Composer Elmer Bernstein gave *The Age of Innocence* its lilting melancholy, the music's soaring, aching strings suggesting the pain tormenting Archer and Olenska. This is never more potent than in the final scene, as Archer's tight expression and closed eyes belie the romantic swirl of Bernstein's score.

In 2002, two years before he died at the age of 82, Bernstein noted of Scorsese, "He has the soul of an artist, so therefore he understands other artists, and you're dealing with him as a colleague artist. More importantly, he has a great appreciation of what music does in film, and not an appreciation from listening to it. He has an appreciation that is based on knowledge. It is not an annoyance to have to change things because his ideas are really interesting, because he really knows what he's doing. That makes the collaboration really interesting."

When they approached the score for *The Age of Innocence*, Scorsese and Bernstein (who had previously collaborated on Scorsese's *Cape Fear* remake) discussed music that would fit the 1870s New York setting.

As Bernstein once explained, "If the music should reflect the period, what class of music so to speak? Should it be popular music, salon music of the time, or serious music of the time? And we went to serious music of the time. It was going to be serious music of the time. How would you represent serious music at 1870? Well, we'll leave out the operatic composers because we're not going to sing through it, so that eliminated Wagner and Verdi, so it left Tchaikovsky. It was a great light, and Johannes Brahms, the other great light. Well, which way do we go, because they're rather different? There's a rather different sensibility between the two composers, and the decision was Brahms. It wasn't anybody making the decision, any one of us—it was us talking together."

When he began writing the score, he worked out of a hotel in London. "I remember writing this stuff in the kitchen of a friend of mine who has a studio in London, and then had a small orchestra, very small orchestra," Bernstein said. "I composed four themes,

ABOVE: In a film where emotions run deep, unexpressed beneath the surface, the music plays an important role.

one of them played two different ways. I came back with that and he picked two of them instantly that he really liked. Now, he likes to have music as he's editing film and right away started to put the music, you know, in the film. He had no other music to begin with. When he was about halfway through the edit, I suggested a procedure, which I wish we could do all the time. I said, 'You know, for a relatively small amount of money, I could go over to Ireland also with a smallish orchestra. Let's pick about twelve pieces, you know, in the film, and I'll go over and we can find out how it's all working.' And we did that in the middle. The company said okay, much to everybody's surprise, and we went over and did that. So, the film and the score were evolving at the same time. It was absolutely ideal."

SUMMARY OF TECHNIQUE

1. RESTRAINT
Daniel Day-Lewis gives a performance of enormous restraint in this final scene. The simplicity of his actions makes his character's sense of duty and resignation all the more poignant and tragic. Likewise, Scorsese's camerawork is subdued, the final image static so that the full impact of its meaning can be absorbed without adornment.

2. JUST THE RIGHT SCORE
Expressive without being flowery, Elmer Bernstein's music underscores the romantic anguish plaguing the characters. At the finale of *The Age of Innocence*, the music says what Newland Archer cannot: we feel the sadness and desolation within him without the character having to speak a word.

3. FLASHBACK
One of the greatest challenges in cinema is to illuminate what a character is thinking. In *The Age of Innocence*, Scorsese brings Archer's inner world to life by flashing back to a pivotal scene earlier in the movie, when the character watched Olenska by the lighthouse. With this flashback, we get a glimpse of Archer's mindset—and a clue to why he makes the decision to walk away. Again, this is all done without dialogue.

4. MYSTERY AND UNHAPPY ENDINGS
It takes a certain amount of courage to resolve *The Age of Innocence* in the way Scorsese does. It's an unhappy ending, but it is the right ending, showing how Newland Archer remained duty-bound, even when others would understand if he didn't. Additionally, the ending doesn't explain itself, instead letting the audience piece together the reasons for the character's behavior. As a result, *The Age of Innocence* is one of Scorsese's most haunting films.

GANGS OF NEW YORK

2002

SCREENPLAY:
Jay Cocks and Steven Zaillian and Kenneth
Lonergan (Story by Jay Cocks)

CINEMATOGRAPHER:
Michael Ballhaus

EDITOR:
Thelma Schoonmaker

PRODUCTION DESIGNER:
Dante Ferretti

PRINCIPAL SCENE ACTORS:
Liam Neeson ("Priest" Vallon)
Daniel Day-Lewis (Bill "The Butcher" Cutting)
John C. Reilly (Happy Jack Mulraney)
Cian McCormack (Young Amsterdam)

SCENE:
The epic Five Points battle

08

I. INTRODUCTION

Of the many genres Martin Scorsese has explored in his career—the dark comedy, the psychological character piece, the thriller, the mob movie, the concert film—he's never made a Western or a war movie. In a sense, the opening of *Gangs of New York* is as close as he's ever come.

Chronicling the mid-nineteenth century rise of New York City, the film is a study of how rival tribes battled for control of the city's Five Points section. These squabbling, lawless gangs are the precursor to the mobsters that populate Scorsese's indelible early movies. "In a sense, this film represents a foundation upon which my other movies are based," he has said. "It creates a world in which the worlds I depicted in *Goodfellas*, *Mean Streets*, *Raging Bull*, and, to a certain extent, *Taxi Driver*, emerge from."

One of *Gangs of New York*'s finest scenes is its grandest and most bloody. At the film's beginning, Young Amsterdam (Cian McCormack) watches as his father, "Priest" Vallon (Liam Neeson), leads his gang the Dead Rabbits (who are Irish immigrants) against Bill "The Butcher" Cutting (Daniel Day-Lewis) and his US-born Natives. An epic hand-to-hand battle ensues in the city square of Five Points as men use meat cleavers, axes, bats, and knives to kill each other, set against a suitably powerful soundtrack and short, increasingly hazy cuts as the snowy ground turns red with blood.

The scene culminates with Bill slaying Priest as Amsterdam looks on; the pain of that moment will linger with Amsterdam for years to come, setting in motion *Gangs of New York*'s principal drama between

the adult Amsterdam (Leonardo DiCaprio)
and the powerful, feared Bill the Butcher.

Scorsese had orchestrated violent scenes
before, but never has one been as lavish and
stylized as *Gangs of New York*'s opening. A
massive undertaking indicative of the movie's
towering ambitions, the scene is brutal, operatic,
and riveting.

OPPOSITE & ABOVE: Bill "The Butcher" Cutting (Daniel
Day-Lewis) and "Priest" Vallon (Liam Neeson) square off
at Five Points in the opening scene of *Gangs of New York*.

II. THE ORIGINS

Gangs of New York finally hit cinemas in the U.S. in December 2002, but it was a film that Scorsese had first conceived more than 30 years earlier.

"When I first met Marty in 1972, he told me that there were two books he wanted to make, *Gangs of New York* and *The Last Temptation of Christ*," Paul Schrader recalled. The idea had entered Scorsese's mind when he stumbled across a book at a friend's house in 1970, the title of which struck a note with him. This was Herbert Asbury's 1928 history of Five Points, *The Gangs of New York*. His early vision for the film was, of course, quite different from the one that would be realized in 30 years. "Think of it like a Western in outer space," Scorsese told his friend, the screenwriter Jay Cocks, at the time. The two of them put a draft together in 1977, and Malcolm McDowell, hot off *A Clockwork Orange* and *If…*, was in line for one of the leading roles, but then came *Raging Bull*, and after the distastrous flop that was the elephantine *Heaven's Gate*, it was looking doubtful that the film would ever get made.

Years passed, but *Gangs* never entirely left Scorsese's mind. While on location for *The Age of Innocence*, he came across a photo from 1896 of a burned-out building, covered with snow and icicles. "I want this to be the first image in my next movie, *Gangs of New York*," he told production designer Dante Ferretti.

Of course, it wasn't his next film. It wasn't until 1998, when rising star Leonardo DiCaprio got hold of the project, and Harvey Weinstein's Miramax were prepared to bankroll it, that the film could at last happen. By this time Scorsese was a different director, and the resulting film very different from the one he might have made in the 1970s, in part due to the actors he was working with, who made their impression on the script and the characters. And Scorsese believes the film would have been more violent, had he made it earlier in his career. After *Casino*, he felt he had said all he had to about the violent act. In *Gangs of New York*, in the battle scenes and amidst all the brutality, the violence is always suggested by the edit, rather than actually shown.

LEFT: A found photograph of a frozen, ruinous house was the inspiration for the look of the opening of *Gangs of New York*.

THE INSPIRATION

To choreograph the chaos of the fight scene, in which myriad different battles are taking place simultaneously, Scorsese turned to Orson Welles' *Chimes at Midnight*. Praising the 1965 movie for containing "the best battle scene put on film," Scorsese has said that he wanted to emulate its technique of intercutting between different individual moments, personalizing the chaos of a massive melee.

"I believe they shot that for many weeks, bits and pieces," Scorsese noted on *Gangs of New York*'s commentary track. "That's what we wound up doing, too: We shot the majority of the opening sequence in three weeks. And then Vic Armstrong, who's an extraordinary action director, he took drawings of mine and basically did them for another six or seven weeks: bits and pieces every day, when the sun was right, with small groups of men."

In *Chimes of Midnight*, Welles managed to convey the scope and carnage of a huge battle. There is a sense of upheaval, but it also feels orchestrated, as if the madness is being organized so that we can comprehend it. *Gangs of New York*'s Five Points scene is similar, illustrating random killings but focusing our attention on the progress of both Bill the Butcher and Priest Vallon, who are destined to square off at the climax.

THIS PAGE: Stills from *Chimes at Midnight*. At top-right, director Orson Welles prepares a shot.

III. DANTE FERRETTI

Gangs of New York's wonderful production design was overseen by Dante Ferretti. He and Scorsese have worked on nine films together to date, and Ferretti, who has won Oscars for *The Aviator*, *Sweeney Todd: The Demon Barber of Fleet Street*, and *Hugo*, is quick to praise the filmmaker. As Ferretti has declared, "I have had three mentors, you could say: Pasolini, Fellini, and Scorsese… They changed my life." Ferretti made his first American film with Scorsese, meeting the director while serving as the production designer on Fellini's *City of Women*. "He is my hero," Ferretti said of Scorsese. "He is a true, true great of the film world… He knew who I was because he knows everything about movies, everything, it's unbelievable."

For *Gangs of New York*, "I had to re-create Five Points and of course none of it exists any more," Ferretti said. "I immersed myself in the period, looking at daguerreotypes, engravings, drawings, the original maps and plans of New York, and I went to see the Ellis Island Immigration Museum. The city I re-created was very accurate, because it was extremely important to be very correct. Initially, we were going to re-create it in Canada, but then we moved to Rome, in part because of the love Martin Scorsese has for Cinecittà studios," the iconic Italian film studio where movies such as *Cleopatra* and *La Dolce Vita* were filmed.

"Dante Ferretti is an incredible perfectionist in every way and a great artist at the same time," *Gangs of New York*'s cinematographer Michael Ballhaus

TOP: Ferretti's illustration of the Five Points area for *Gangs of New York*.

ABOVE: An illustration of Five Points from 1829.

WORKING TOGETHER

Of Dante Ferretti's set, cinematographer Michael Ballhaus remarked, "It was like stepping into another world—everything was done so precisely, every square foot was lovingly furnished. It was incredible. We were able to shoot just as if we were on location, looking in all directions, even though we were on a studio lot."

When you have a set as complete as the one Ferretti built for *Gangs of New York*, you want to use it to its full potential. For the dramatic closing shot of the Five Points scene, a camera was rigged to a cable, using two construction cranes and a Range Rover to draw it up to a height of 46 meters (150 feet) to show the whole of the set and beyond (which would later be filled in using CG).

observed. "He supervises every detail, even if it doesn't appear in the film. You can shoot every square inch of his sets in a 360-degree radius from floor to ceiling… Since I am such an admirer of Dante's work, I love to show as much of his sets as possible. I literally try to bring his sets to life."

Around 250 people worked to build the lavish sets of *Gangs of New York*, and Ferretti would receive an Oscar nomination for his efforts, but Ferretti's belief is that he's really servicing another person's aspirations. "I think the job of the production designer is always to construct a world that belongs to the director—to be in harmony with him and give form to his vision," Ferretti said. "The way I start is always with the director. He calls me. I am normally the first one in."

BELOW: A still from the film shows the set as it appeared.

BOTTOM: The set in production.

LEFT: Preparing for bloodshed: the opening scene of *Gangs of New York* sets the tone for the whole movie.

IV. THE LOOK

It's not shocking that violence is a major component of *Gangs of New York*, and of this scene in particular, but Scorsese wanted to approach it in a new way. "I've done violence in pretty flat and straightforward ways," he once said. "I didn't know how else to do it but, by the end of *Casino* with the killing of Joe Pesci and his brother, in my mind, I thought it was important to depict the downside of that lifestyle. You have to be honest in the portrayal of violence."

The Five Points scene has a mournful quality, although it's dynamically constructed. In part that's because Scorsese, with typically inspired musical choices, uses a haunting instrumental from Peter Gabriel, "Signal to Noise," to score the sequence. But it's also because the gruesome acts of butchery are hinted at rather than shown. In the commentary track that accompanies the film's DVD, Scorsese explained that he wanted to show "the completions of actions," rather than the sight of, say, knives going into bodies, so that the violence was suggested.

"Violence was an everyday occurrence [in the mid-nineteenth century in New York]—of all kinds, domestic, street, gangland, everything." Scorsese explained. "It's so much a part of the fabric of the film you had to find a way to give an impression of that without constantly dwelling on it."

Similarly, Ballhaus explained how different frame rates were used in these scenes to vary the action: "We shot some battle scenes at eight frames per second; sometimes we step-printed them four times to create a strobing effect, and other times we didn't print them up," Ballhaus told *American Cinematographer*. "We often used speed changes—going from 24 fps to 30 or 32 fps—to underscore significant moments. Marty created a similar effect with editing patterns as well."

The sequence leaves you squeamish, but it is artfully constructed, with the slowing down and speeding up of certain actions through the shooting, and the allusions to carnage rather than the display of it in the edit.

"There's a lot more coverage in this film than Marty and I normally do," said Ballhaus, whose son Florian was the cinematographer for the second-unit work. "But on a movie of this size you have to cover yourself and think ahead. This was actually the best experience I've ever had with a second unit—they shot a lot of material, and it matched our material perfectly."

KEEPING IT REAL

Gangs of New York was one of Scorsese's most difficult shoots. "Everybody was exhausted," he later recalled. "There were conflicts all around. We had language problems … we were running out of money. The pressure to finish. People were leaving, props were being taken away. Extras were leaving. We still had to shoot certain things and I wasn't sure we could shoot them with only three people or whoever was left. We managed, but it was hard."

Part of that agony came from the shoot's commitment to realism, including the massive, expensive physical production incorporating Ferretti's square-mile recreation of Five Points. "I have to feel the period. I don't like to copy—I want to be like an actor, to become part of the film," Ferretti explained. "I want to feel like an architect who lived in the period, and I make the things that he would make, even down to the mistakes. That gives me a freedom, but always inside the story, inside the period."

Of course, there are cheaper, easier ways of accomplishing these tasks, but they aren't always better. "I remember once George Lucas came to see me on the set of *Gangs of New York*," Ferretti said, "and he remarked that everything could be done on the green screen. That is true, but I do think that actors give much more when they perform in real surroundings."

Still, *Gangs of New York* had to resort to CG in a pinch. Harvey Weinstein, a producer on the film, recalled in 2013 that one scene required an elephant, which never arrived. On the day of the shoot, Weinstein had to get creative: "I called George Lucas and said, 'We're effed. We don't have a goddamn elephant. Tell us how to shoot it!' …They told us how to shoot it and how to create the elephant walking through the streets… Here's George Lucas telling us how to shoot this goddamn thing!"

BELOW: Ferretti's huge set included a one-mile-square recreation of the Five Points neighborhood, a Chinese-style theater/brothel, and a waterfront area with real ships, shown here. In the background you can see one of cranes used to capture the set from all angles.

V. VIC ARMSTRONG

Vic Armstrong is a legendary stunt coordinator and director who has worked with Steven Spielberg, Paul Verhoeven, and George Lucas. (He was also Harrison Ford's stunt double for many years.) To complete the epic Five Points battle sequence in *Gangs of New York*, Scorsese turned to Armstrong to be his second unit director.

"Vic Armstrong is, of course, a legend in the film world, in the tradition of the great Yakima Canutt," the director once declared. For the Five Points scene, Scorsese would give Armstrong drawings of what he wanted him to film. But he also wanted Armstrong to see silent films from famed Russian directors like Alexander Dovzhenko, Sergei Eisenstein, and Vsevolod Pudovkin. "I'm always fascinated by Russian montage," Scorsese has explained. "I happen to like editing, particularly montage in the 1920s."

Armstrong was responsible for coordinating and shooting the sequence, working with drawings Scorsese had made. The main part of the battle was completed in roughly three weeks.

Later acknowledging that the Five Points sequence was the biggest he'd worked on to that point, Armstrong wrote in his memoir, *The True Adventures of the World's Greatest Stuntman*, "I planned the whole battle sequence and worked with Marty shooting it. Then he left to carry on with studio interiors while I mopped up all the assorted bits of carnage, like ripping people's faces open and breaking kneecaps."

BELOW LEFT: Legendary stuntman and *Gangs of New York*'s second unit director Vic Armstrong plunges into the freezing water of Glacier Bay, Alaska, as a stuntman on *Bear Island* in 1979.

BELOW RIGHT: Armstrong helped Scorsese coordinate the action in this epic fight scene.

WHAT'S A SECOND UNIT DIRECTOR?

Armstrong's job on *Gangs of New York* isn't one that many film viewers understand. The second unit director is the person who oversees secondary shots on a film, often working with actors who aren't the main stars. (For an action movie, the second unit director normally handles the set pieces, conferring with the stunt actors.) The job requires, among others things, the ability to mimic the look of the principal director's shots. It also means being willing to adhere to the filmmaker's direction rather than imposing one's own style on the proceedings.

"You're second unit director—you're not main unit director—[and] you have to bend to their wishes and you're going to do what they want, you know?" Armstrong said in 2011. "Because you are their second set of eyes. That is one of the hardest parts of second unit, copying somebody's style, because it has to match seamlessly, visually, and also delivering the best action you can. You know, you walk along hot coals a lot of the time, and it's quite a political situation, but it's part of the job, you know?"

SUMMARY OF TECHNIQUE

1. EMBRACING THE REAL

Gangs of New York required the building of real sets. Though it was a hard, expensive shoot, Scorsese's commitment to authenticity gives the film a scope and grandeur. Of course, even a low-budget project can embrace realism to ground the proceedings and provide an air of believability.

2. ORDER OUT OF CHAOS

The Five Points sequence is a jumble of bodies and weapons shown in quick flashes. Scorsese both amplifies that chaos and creates order out of it. Intense cutaways to individual confrontations add heft to the overall battle sequence, personalizing the action so that we feel the individual deaths.

3. SHOOTING MORE THAN YOU NEED

With a sequence so elaborate, it's important to err on the side of too much coverage, rather than risk not having enough. Led by the example of *Chimes at Midnight*, Scorsese shot the Five Points sequence for weeks, storyboarding the action in advance so that he had an idea of what he wanted. The extensive coverage gave Scorsese and editor Thelma Schoonmaker plenty of options in post-production.

4. SETTING THE TONE

The Five Points battle scene doesn't just kick off *Gangs of New York*: it sets the tone for everything that follows, establishing the central conflict between Bill the Butcher and Amsterdam, but also preparing the audience for the violence that's to come. Scorsese stages the sequence beautifully, laying out the ambition of his project while starting off with a bang. Character, theme, and mood are all laid out through action, not dialogue.

THE DEPARTED

2006

SCREENPLAY:
William Monahan (Based on *Infernal Affairs*,
screenplay by Alan Mak and Felix Chong)

CINEMATOGRAPHER:
Michael Ballhaus

EDITOR:
Thelma Schoonmaker

PRODUCTION DESIGNER:
Kristi Zea

PRINCIPAL SCENE ACTORS:
Leonardo DiCaprio (Billy Costigan)
Jack Nicholson (Frank Costello)
Ray Winstone (Mr. French)

SCENE:
Billy Costigan meets Frank Costello

I. INTRODUCTION

ABOVE: DiCaprio's Billy Costigan is the undercover police officer cast adrift in *The Departed*.

A violent, amoral, foul-mouthed crime-thriller lacking any of the trappings of a "prestige picture," *The Departed* isn't a traditional Best Picture Oscar winner. But the movie that finally netted Martin Scorsese his first Academy Award (for Best Director) may be the director's most purely entertaining, energetic, and funny.

Scorsese consciously kept himself and his cast from imitating *Infernal Affairs*, the 2002 Hong Kong thriller directed by Andrew Lau and Alan Mak that inspired *The Departed*. Though his remake is relatively faithful to the original, Scorsese knew he couldn't try to replicate that film's kinetic style. "Marty refused to see [*Infernal Affairs*], because he didn't want us influenced by it," cinematographer Michael Ballhaus would later recall. "He wanted to make his own character-driven movie."

Indeed, Scorsese focused on the themes of screenwriter William Monahan's adaptation. "I didn't think of it as Hong Kong," Scorsese said at the time of *The Departed*, which was set in Boston, later adding, "I liked the idea ... the concept of the two informers. [I am] totally, whether I like or not, drawn to stories

that have to do with trust and betrayal. I found that I kept being drawn back to the script and to the project. It became something else."

The Departed was also, by all accounts, a difficult film to make, with a rushed shooting schedule and a particularly impulsive actor among the production obstacles. And yet, *The Departed* succeeds, in part because of those realities. This is a movie that churns with frantic, paranoid energy, perhaps unconsciously reflecting the breakneck speed in which it was made.

"Sometimes a picture gets away from you and sometimes it doesn't," the filmmaker said. "What I felt about the first four weeks of shooting *The Departed* was that it was not going smoothly, it was not going as planned." Scorsese turned a corner, though, and what came out was a movie of rambunctious performances and unpredictable outbursts. This was never truer than in the first meeting of two of *The Departed*'s central characters: the undercover cop Billy Costigan (Leonardo DiCaprio) and the crime boss Frank Costello (Jack Nicholson). It's a scene that's filled with danger and dark humor. It feels like it could detonate at any moment—or fall apart.

LEFT & BELOW: Scenes from the stylish and powerful *Infernal Affairs*.

ABOVE: A light moment on the set of *The Departed*.

II. JACK ATTACK

An elaborate crime film with two separate characters —Billy Costigan and Matt Damon's Colin Sullivan— living double lives, *The Departed* had its own drama behind the scenes. Michael Ballhaus, the film's cinematographer, once remarked, "[Scorsese] wanted to push the envelope, while keeping in mind we were working with major movie stars … on a $100-million Hollywood movie. Our schedule was pushed forward by about half a year because of the actors' schedules, so Marty didn't have as much time as he wanted in preparation. We also only had Jack [Nicholson] for five weeks, so we had to squeeze all of his scenes into that period. That was very hard for Marty, because he loves to shoot in sequence."

Nicholson wasn't on the set for much of *The Departed*—roughly only a quarter of the film's 99 shooting days—but he's unquestionably the film's dynamic center, playing the ferocious, arrogant mobster Frank Costello. A powerful and charismatic personality, Nicholson apparently engaged in a bit of a power struggle with Scorsese during the shoot. Nicholson "had changes made in the script, practically rewriting it," Ballhaus revealed. "The problem was he not only broadened and made his own role bigger, he actually cut back the other characters' roles."

But though Nicholson may have been difficult to work with at times, he was clearly also a galvanizing presence, and his intensity perfect for the role of Frank Costello. "When Jack came on the set he would do things that were just nuts," Damon told the *Telegraph* around the film's release. "If you look at Leo and I in all our scenes with Jack, we are like

ABOVE: Jack Nicholson with Matt Damon on the set.

the set every day expecting the unexpected. He is going to throw curveballs at you and you have to be completely prepared for anything. There was tons of improvisation with him. I was never sure which side of Costello he was going to be playing on any particular day. It makes you terrified as an actor, and it ups the stakes."

That live-wire intensity is embodied in the scene where Costigan is introduced to Costello, the mobster briefly bonding with the kid before having his goon Mr. French (Ray Winstone) break open his cast to make sure he's not wearing a wire. Costello goes from warm to menacing without betraying a hint of emotion: He's an unfeeling, psychopathic monster ready to strike at any moment.

deer caught in the headlights." In the same profile piece, DiCaprio said, "He's a force of nature and you have to be prepared to roll with the punches. There were moments during filming when I didn't know what was going to happen next. If you hire Jack Nicholson to play an Irish Mob kingpin in a Martin Scorsese film of this genre he's going to make the role his own and that involves going into

"Jack is very interesting because he will stay that way off camera, in the daytime and nighttime —always coming up with ideas, always pushing and shoving to the point where the other people in the picture come up to that level," Scorsese once said. "That's where you experiment a lot, you try things. He was always inventive. We knew we had to embrace this character in a different way from other characters like him on other movies I've made."

GENUINE FEAR

In one notorious scene rife with tension, Billy Costigan meets Costello at a restaurant, where Costello accuses Costigan of being a rat. Although the shoot seemed to go well, Nicholson said afterward to Scorsese that he didn't think that DiCaprio's character was scared enough. They had some extra time the following day and decided to take another shot at it. DiCaprio recalled that before he went into the shoot, "[the] prop guy, on the way to the set, said, 'I just want to let you know something for safety purposes that Mr. Nicholson has a bottle of whiskey, some matches, and a gun. I just have to tell you that.'"

All the anxiety, the air of unpredictability that makes this moment so gripping, was real; like his character, DiCaprio genuinely had no idea what was going to happen next—and that's part of what makes this scene, and the movie, so thrilling to watch.

III. DICAPRIO & SCORSESE

ABOVE: Leonardo DiCaprio and Martin Scorsese making *The Departed*.

It was while he working with Robert De Niro on *This Boy's Life* in 1993 that De Niro recommended Leonardo DiCaprio to Scorsese, but it was seeing his performance in *What's Eating Gilbert Grape* a little later, when the film came out on television, that Scorsese was convinced about the young actor, and he remembered De Niro's phonecall. Scorsese's last collaboration with De Niro was *Casino* in 1995, and they no longer had the closeness of their early collaborations. Then DiCaprio became involved in *Gangs of New York*, the film that Scorsese had first written a script for twenty years earlier in 1976. DiCaprio wanted to work with Scorsese, Scorsese wanted to work with DiCaprio, and he wanted to make *Gangs of New York*. It was perfect timing.

The Departed was DiCaprio's third collaboration with Scorsese. (To date, they have made five films

together.) Over that time, the filmmaker has watched the box-office star and five-time Oscar nominee evolve as an actor.

"Having worked with Leo in *Gangs of New York* and *The Aviator*, I sense something about him," Scorsese said upon the release of *The Departed*. "There's a great deal emotionally going on inside of him. For me it was interesting—I felt comfortable with the emotional process he was going through, and it reminded me very much of De Niro. It was a different frame of reference: I'm thirty years older, but he approached emotional subjects in a very similar way and he also thinks about things in life the way I do... There's no doubt that he was a boy when we did *Gangs of New York*, which is what I wanted. But when he did Howard Hughes in *The Aviator*, that changed everything."

Naturally, because Scorsese was for so long associated with Robert De Niro, it's inevitable that comparisons will be made between DiCaprio and De Niro. For DiCaprio's part, his love of Scorsese started with De Niro.

"I'm a fan of [Scorsese's] work, number one," DiCaprio once said about the appeal, for him, of working with the filmmaker. "Truth is, I suppose, for me anyway, that it all started wanting to work with him doing *This Boy's Life* with Robert De Niro and getting sort of familiar with Robert De Niro's work and obviously that means Martin Scorsese's work as well. So I became a fan of his work at a very early age… I don't have an exciting term for it other than we have a good time working together and we have similar tastes as far as the films we like.

THIS PAGE: Leonardo DiCaprio and Martin Scorsese over the years: (clockwise from top left) in *Gangs of New York*, *The Aviator*, *Shutter Island*, and *The Wolf of Wall Street*.

He certainly has broadened my spectrum as far as films that are out there in the history of cinema and the importance of cinema. And it really brought me to different levels as an actor. I look at him as a mentor."

Despite the well-documented difficulties in making the film, for both actor and director the decision to do it was an easy one, and it began with Monahan's script. "I got the script around when Marty got the script and we just talked to each other. It was one of those things that we really didn't need to discuss. He really wanted to do it; I really wanted to do it," DiCaprio said.

IV. EDITING

For several decades, Scorsese has closely collaborated with editor Thelma Schoonmaker. (In the process, she has won three Oscars cutting his movies.) Along the way, they've developed an approach in which complete continuity isn't always obeyed: a head may be slightly turned from one shot to another, or items on a table may not be in the same arrangement between cuts.

This tolerance of what some would perceive to be errors, frowned upon by classical filmmakers, gives a movie like *The Departed* an unhinged energy, creating an uneasy tension in scenes that are already sufficiently stressful because of their intrigue. And Schoonmaker, who was married to the late Michael Powell, part of the directing team (alongside Emeric Pressburger) that made films such as *The Life and Death of Colonel Blimp* and *The Red Shoes*, has never cared about following strict continuity rules.

"The priority is absolutely on the best take for performance, and frankly I don't understand why people get so hung up on these [continuity] issues," she has said, "because if you look at films throughout history, you will see enormous continuity errors everywhere… Even in *The Red Shoes*, a film that nobody ever has complaints about, there are enormous continuity bumps, and it doesn't matter. You know why? Because you're being carried along by the power of the film."

Due to the film's problematic shoot, much of the graft was done in post-production, and many structural changes were made at this point. The

ABOVE: Martin Scorsese lines up the next shot.

BELOW LEFT: Thelma Schoonmaker with Martin Scorsese in front of the memorial plaque for Michael Powell and Emeric Pressburger at their work base in Dorset House, London.

BELOW RIGHT: Thelma Schoonmaker with Martin Scorsese (behind), Richard Pierce, and Michael Wadleigh during the filming of *Woodstock* (1970).

THE STRUGGLES

"We had to struggle with that movie," editor Thelma Schoonmaker said in late 2013 about *The Departed.* "We had a lot of writing problems and structural problems, but that happens on a lot of films and that's part of your job [as an editor]."

Rushed into production to accommodate the A-list cast's busy schedules, the film didn't experience the smoothest sailing, but Scorsese's veteran collaborators like Schoonmaker learned to adjust.

"The film wasn't storyboarded, but we were well prepared," cinematographer Michael Ballhaus once recalled. "We knew the shots we wanted, and finished on time every day. Marty had to recast one actor after shooting with him for five days. We redid those scenes with a new actor in two days."

"*The Departed* came out the way I wanted it to come out," Scorsese told film critic Richard Schickel. "But it cost a lot of money, and there were big-name stars in it, and therefore I had to work with the studio very closely. Screen it, argue, discuss it, you know… The thing is, I don't know if it's worth going through the process again. Because, ultimately, the marketplace for big-budget films means there will be less experimentation in them."

The film would win four Academy Awards and grossed about $290 million worldwide. But when Scorsese was wrapping the project, there was no way to know how it would be received. And perhaps he didn't even care by that point. "When I was finishing *The Departed*, I said, 'I'm out of here,'" he told Schickel. "I barely saw the answer print."

editor has to really know the story and the script to create something as masterful as *The Departed.* "It's an editor's job to create tension, drama, shock, emotion, and surprise," Schoonmaker said, and sometimes, as in *The Departed*, this means cutting up the script or changing the focus the better to tell the story. Despite the "errors," Schoonmaker's work was deservedly lauded, and she won her third Oscar for *The Departed.*

TOP LEFT: *The Departed* was the seventh time that Michael Ballhaus and Martin Scorsese worked on a film together.

BOTTOM LEFT: Martin Scorsese is flanked by Michael Ballhaus and Jack Nicholson while working on *The Departed.*

V. THE LOOK

As vivid as *The Departed*'s characters and violence are, so too is the film's look. "At one point, he planned to do it in black and white, but the studio wouldn't agree," remembered Michael Ballhaus. "We spoke about doing a Digital Intermediate and desaturating and changing colors a bit and making some scenes colder with a little more contrast."

As always with Scorsese, he also supplied his cinematographer with reference films, and in the case of *The Departed* that meant looking at 1940s noirs like *T-Men* and *Raw Deal*, while also examining recent Asian cinema such as *Oldboy* and *Bad Guy*. "Marty wanted a noir feel, and [cinematographer John] Alton's work is really wonderful and atmospheric," Ballhaus told *American Cinematographer*. "By asking me to also watch those wild Asian movies, I think Marty was pushing me to try something different. I tried to do that, but after a couple of days on the shoot I realized that although the styles of those movies were great for the particular stories they were telling, we were doing an American movie

BELOW & BOTTOM: Scorsese drew on inspirations for *The Departed*, from black-and-white noirs to modern Asian cinema, including *Raw Deal* starring Dennis O'Keefe and Claire Trevor (below), and *Oldboy*, starring Choi Min-sik and Ji-Tae Yu (Yu pictured at bottom).

with American stars. In the end, I had to pull back a bit from those wilder styles; I couldn't go that far with this movie."

Ballhaus also learned a lot from studying *Infernal Affairs*—rather than seeking to replicate the look, he notes that it taught him a lot about what he wanted to do and what he didn't want. A more character-driven study than the original, it was important to Ballhaus that, though the film should have darkness, the characters should never be lost in it.

SPOT THE X

Throughout his movies, Scorsese uses visual references to add another layer of meaning. For *The Departed*, he borrowed a reference from 1932's gangster classic *Scarface*: X-shapes were incorporated into the lighting and set design to signify moments of menace and danger. Chief lighting technician Andy Day told *American Cinematographer* how the whole crew got involved. "The X motif was something everyone worked really hard to achieve. We even had grips and electricians saying, 'Hey, we could put an X here!' Michael was always very excited if someone found another place to put an X. He and Marty did it partially as a homage to the great noir films, and also to create a sense of imminent doom."

ABOVE: The original 1932 *Scarface*, directed by Howard Hawks and Richard Rosson, starring Paul Muni as Tony.

SUMMARY OF TECHNIQUE

1. MAKING YOUR OWN FILM
Scorsese insisted on not copying *Infernal Affairs*, recognizing that his skills as a filmmaker were different than those of directors Andrew Lau and Alan Mak. Instead, he focused on his own thematic interests, in the process making a film that is reminiscent of the original but very much a product of his particular DNA.

2. AN AIR OF UNPREDICTABILITY
Casting Jack Nicholson meant that *The Departed* wouldn't have a modest, understated performance at its center. But the movie responds to the actor's high-wire energy, producing a series of alert, anxious performances around him that are in keeping with the film's paranoid thrust. And even though the crew didn't have as much time to prepare as they would have liked because of a sped-up production schedule, they were ready to face the challenge. Even a veteran director like Scorsese, who prefers shooting in sequence, has to adjust his methods when the situation requires it.

3. BREAKING THE RULES
Thelma Schoonmaker's editing throughout *The Departed* isn't "correct" because it breaks continuity rules. But look at the effect it achieves, suggesting a tension within the scenes that mirrors the characters' own. Sometimes, not following cinematic rules can lead to fresh approaches to storytelling.

4. DRAWING FROM THE PAST
To prepare for the shoot, Scorsese gave cinematographer Michael Ballhaus films from the 1940s to study. *The Departed* doesn't have the tone of those classic noirs, but it embodies their spirit of no-nonsense, stripped-down filmmaking. One doesn't need to mimic established films—what's important is to absorb their lessons.

HUGO
2011

SCREENPLAY:
John Logan (Based on the book
The Invention of Hugo Cabret by Brian Selznick)

CINEMATOGRAPHER:
Robert Richardson

EDITOR:
Thelma Schoonmaker

PRODUCTION DESIGNER:
Dante Ferretti

PRINCIPAL SCENE ACTORS:
Ben Kingsley (Georges Méliès)
Helen McCrory (Mama Jeanne)

SCENE:
The Georges Méliès flashback

I. INTRODUCTION

It probably came as a surprise to some that Martin Scorsese would make a family film. And that this film would be in 3D. But *Hugo* proved to be a more personal and emotional project for the director than might be initially suspected—for two reasons. The first is that Scorsese was the father of a young daughter, and he thought it might be good to make a movie that, unlike most of the rest of his oeuvre, she'd be old enough to watch. From that notion came an adaptation of Brian Selznick's 2007 illustrated children's book *The Invention of Hugo Cabret*, which tells the story of an orphan boy named Hugo (Asa Butterfield) who lives in a train station in Paris in the early 1930s.

But the Dickens-like tale appealed to Scorsese for another reason, too. Mourning his dead father, Hugo obsessively tries to repair an automaton that he and his dad discovered; the boy touchingly hopes that by bringing the automaton to life, he can keep the connection with his father alive as well. But when the machine starts working again,

it generates a cryptic message that sends Hugo and his new friend Isabelle (Chloë Grace Moretz) on a quest that leads them to her godfather, the renowned former filmmaker Georges Méliès (Ben Kingsley).

And it's here where *Hugo* is at its most poignant. For as much as Hugo is an orphan, so too is Méliès, a magician who became entranced by the possibilities of cinema and decided to become a director, only to watch his films fall out of favor once World War I consumed Europe. Hugo is trying to find a home in *Hugo*, and likewise Méliès wants to reconnect with the creative passion that once made him unspeakably happy. Scorsese makes that love of cinema's possibilities manifest—particularly in a vivid flashback sequence near the end of *Hugo* where Méliès relates his earlier life as a filmmaker. If *Hugo* is a children's film, it's also Scorsese's way of proselytizing an art form he wants to pass along to a new generation. It's a movie about the childlike joy of cinema, made by someone who's never lost that sense of wonder.

LEFT: Ben Kingsley as the young Méliès alongside his son, Edmund Kingsley, during the flashback scene in *Hugo*.

OPPOSITE: Ben Kingsley as Georges Méliès takes a bow.

II. FROM PAGE TO SCREEN

ABOVE: Scorsese shows Brian Selznick's illustrations from *The Invention of Hugo Cabret* to the film's young stars.

Although *Hugo* salutes cinema's lasting legacy, the book that inspired the film wanted to preserve the value of other art forms, too. In his foreword to the published screenplay, *The Invention of Hugo Cabret* author Brian Selznick noted, "[The book] was intended to celebrate the history of cinema and to celebrate Méliès, one of its greatest and most overlooked pioneers. But really, for me, it's about the importance of books. In fact, the book itself, the object in your hand when you are reading my original story, is actually an important part of the plot. As a result, I thought the book I made was unfilmable. But then Martin Scorsese called! That's when I first thought to myself, 'Hmmm, maybe this can work on the screen.'"

That love for books is still reflected in *Hugo*: Hugo and Isabelle talk excitedly about Jules Verne stories and Robin Hood adventures. But partly because of the medium in which it was made, *Hugo*

overwhelmingly honors the scope and imagination of movies. And even Selznick's book itself has a cinematic grandeur. Working with black-and-white pencil drawings, the author illustrated *Hugo Cabret* almost as if they were storyboards, especially the early establishing scenes of Paris and the train station. Speaking with the *Guardian* in 2012, Selznick said, "The [film's] camera movements are based on my drawings, but bigger, grander, and more operatic than anything I could have imagined."

The adaptation took several years to get off the ground, and screenwriter John Logan, who had previously collaborated with Scorsese on *The Aviator*, focused on finding the right direction for the film. "Give the book to five different screenwriters, and you will get five different versions of the story, five different movies," Logan once wrote about the *Hugo* experience. "So what was it about the book that touched me?" After talking with Scorsese, they

ABOVE: Hugo and Isabelle first discover Méliès' secret history within the pages of a book. At bottom, Michael Stuhlbarg plays Rene Tabard, the fictitious film enthusiast who shows the children Méliès' glorious *A Trip to the Moon*.

realized that they were both drawn to Hugo's plaintive eyes in Selznick's illustrations. "We began to circle an idea: a film of damaged characters that are finally healed by their courage, their imagination, and their compassion."

Recalling his own first time reading *Hugo Cabret*, Scorsese said in 2012, "I had one of those experiences you often hear about. I was given the book about four years ago and sat down and read it completely in one sitting. I immediately connected to the story. When I was reading I didn't realize the man in the toy store would be Georges Méliès. Then I discovered it was a true story. He worked in the toy store for sixteen years because he was broke and someone did discover him."

CHILDHOOD STIRRINGS

Occasionally, Martin Scorsese takes a long time getting comfortable with a project before he finally decides to take it on. (For instance, Robert De Niro had to campaign for years on *Raging Bull* and *The King of Comedy*; *Gangs of New York* had to wait two decades before all the elements would come together.) But for *Hugo*, the filmmaker took to the material almost immediately, in part because of his daughter.

"When I received the [book] from [producer] Graham King my wife read it," Scorsese recalled. "She loved it and gave it to me and I read it… It was a graphic novel in a sense from the look of it. But, also I have a young daughter. I guess it was two trains running in a way. I was with my daughter every day and I just began to see things differently and perceive life or the world around one in a child's view as it changes and the imagination of a child, the creativity of a child, but also a child's thoughts and storytelling. So, it just seemed to be a very happy coincidence that this story … resolves itself through the device of motion pictures. Graham King said, 'Marty, this is you. You have to do it.' It all came together."

But that didn't mean that Scorsese wanted to make *Hugo* as a traditional fantasy film, despite incorporating green screens and 3D: "It's not a *Chronicles of Narnia* or a *Harry Potter* or *Lord of the Rings* type of fantasy. I would define that kind of fantasy as having viscerality. You're intended to perceive events or people as very, very real. A dragon appears outside a window, and you can imagine it coming into the room, with blue flames and beautiful green emeralds for eyes. With *Hugo*, the fantasy is very real, but it's in your head and in your heart. It has to do with the mechanisms—whether it's the clocks, the interiors, the locomotives, the trains, the automaton—with the inner workings of these objects."

ABOVE LEFT: Hugo and Isabelle discover a little magic.

III. 3D

The decision to shoot the film in 3D was embraced early on in preproduction. As cinematographer Robert Richardson, who won his third Academy Award for *Hugo*, explained, "There is a narrative movement within the book where words step seamlessly into illustrations and the illustrations continue the narrative. I believe Marty's decision to produce *Hugo* in 3D was based upon his desire to provide the most proficient and inspirational translation of the source material for the audience."

"The book was designed to imitate what a movie camera can do," Selznick has said. "It was very consciously thinking about movies and editing and zooming in and zooming out and panning and all of these camera movements. But I was doing it in service of a book. To see it how closely Marty stuck with all of my drawing sequences—the drawings that I did that imitated storyboards became storyboards for a Martin Scorsese movie. When I was on set, everybody had a copy of the book. [Production designer] Dante Ferretti based all the sets on my book. It was like I was collaborating with everyone."

"It was a given that we were to produce the film in digital format," Richardson told *British*

Cinematographer. "There was very little discussion about that. The question that we discussed was whether to shoot in 2D and convert to 3D after the film is edited, or the alternative, on-set capture in 3D. We chose on-set capture in 3D. The principal reason for that decision was that the results were immediately visible to all through 3D monitors. That enabled Marty to decide whether to alter shots to make better use of 3D, including subtracting or enhancing the physical space and acting."

But working in 3D wasn't simply an issue that would affect the film's cinematography. Ferretti, who also won his third Oscar for *Hugo*, commented, "There were big sets, a lot of crew. But it was tough and intense, because it was also my first movie in 3D. And 3D makes a difference, yes, for sure. Everything is alive in 3D, so if you put something in the foreground you see you have more depth to it, but not really to the shot itself. The set decorator needs to work in a different way—we did some tests before and we realized you have to put more things in the foreground. But I loved it; actually, I just loved it."

For Scorsese, the decision to go with 3D wasn't just an aesthetic choice but, also, a return to the

ABOVE: Asa Butterfield hangs out in a scene from *Hugo*.

moviegoing pleasures of his youth. "I've been a 3D fan since I was 12, in 1953," he said, "and I saw every 3D film at that time: *It Came From Outer Space, Creature From the Black Lagoon, Kiss Me, Kate,* which is quite beautiful in 3D. What I really responded to was the figures, the people in the frame. You have a lot of that in *Dial M for Murder.* In *Kiss Me, Kate,* there's a shot where Ann Miller moves toward the camera with a fan as she dances. You feel as if you're onstage right next to her. It's a different experience, completely. Different from theater, different from 2D film. It just is."

However, Scorsese didn't want his foray into 3D with *Hugo* to suggest that he thought all films now needed the technology. "Generally, whenever there's a new technological development, there's a corresponding sense of excitement," he said after *Hugo*'s release. "The same thing happened with the introduction of three-strip Technicolor and CinemaScope, and Dolby. And then everyone remembers it's only a means, not an end. Real 3D is beautiful, but it's just one choice, one tool among many, and you only want to use it if it's the right tool."

ABOVE: (From top) *Kiss Me, Kate, It Came From Outer Space,* and *Dial M for Murder*—some of the 1950s 3D films that inspired Scorsese's use of it in *Hugo*.

IV. THE LOOK

Georges Méliès wasn't just an important character in *Hugo*—his movies also became a guide for the film's visual palette, as did the movies that had influenced him. "In respect to colors and look, it was Marty's idea to use Autochrome for inspiration," Robert Richardson once said. "It was an early form of color photography where the plates or negatives were coated with starch dyes. The Lumière brothers patented the process in 1903."

However, Richardson noted, "It is not possible to re-create that look in digital format in the strictest sense, but we were inspired by viewing Autochrome plates in various museums as well as what has been reproduced in books. The pictures in books are an approximation, and of great value, but the actual plates are superior. There were 3D Autochromes, or what at that time were called Stereoscopic. We didn't try to replicate the Autochrome look. We used it as a basis for creating a look for *Hugo*."

As we learn in Hugo's flashbacks, narrated by Kingsley, Méliès first became entranced by movies by going to see Auguste and Louis Lumière's *The Arrival of a Train at La Ciotat* (*L'arrivée d'un train en gare de La Ciotat*). *Hugo* references the popular belief that audiences ran screaming from the moving image when the 50-second film was first screened in 1896. Although this is an urban legend, the film and indeed the myth of it suggest the storytelling and illusionary possibilities of cinema in its earliest days.

The homage to Méliès is apparent in the film's flashbacks and dream sequences, with their vivid, hyper-real colors. "[Hugo's] memories have a distinct look that was driven by the research we did about Autochrome," said Richardson, while "[t]he look of his dreams were inspired by another early color process … tinting and toning. Georges Méliès, who was a pioneer of substantial substance in the history of filmmaking, used hand-tinting in some films."

TOP & MIDDLE: In *Hugo*, memories and dream sequences have a distinct look, influenced by processes contemporary to the film's setting and inspired by the work of early pioneers of filmmaking, such as the Lumière brothers (middle) and Méliès himself.

BOTTOM: The Lumières' *The Arrival of a Train at La Ciotat.*

WHO WAS GEORGES MÉLIÈS?

No doubt one of the side benefits Scorsese hoped to achieve with *Hugo* was bringing more awareness to the forgotten pioneer of film, Georges Méliès.

"What's amazing about Méliès is that he explored and invented pretty much everything that we're doing now," Scorsese said upon *Hugo*'s release. "It is in a direct line, all the way, from the sci-fi and fantasy films of the '30s, '40s, and '50s, up to the work of Harryhausen, Spielberg, Lucas, James Cameron. It's all there. Méliès did what we do now with computer, green screen, and digital, only he did it in his camera at his studio."

Born in 1861, Méliès was born into a family that ran a profitable shoe company. He didn't go into the business, though; instead, he was attracted to the stage, especially magic shows. Becoming an illusionist, he soon recognized that movies could give him a platform to deliver his magic on a bigger canvas.

As the flashback sequence in *Hugo* shows, Méliès built his own camera and began making films, casting his wife as one of their stars. The extended sequence has a fantastical air that feels almost magical; the playful, almost innocent tone capturing the seemingly unlimited possibility of this new art form. Kingsley and McCrory give warm, likeable performances, as if they're living a dream that, the audience knows, can't last.

In the flashbacks, we see Méliès constructing his special effects—such as making characters "disappear" on screen—as he shoots his movies in his private studio. "The most enjoyable time was building an approximation of Georges Méliès's glass studio," Scorsese told the *New York Times*. "We started replicating scenes from Méliès films as best we could. We recreated the underwater set for *Kingdom of the Fairies*. With Méliès's films, especially the hand-colored ones, it's like illuminated manuscripts come alive. We shot Méliès shooting his films for five or six days. It was one of the best times I've had shooting a picture."

That translates on the screen: *Hugo* is a joyous look at the magic of moviemaking. And although the real Méliès wasn't rediscovered in such a wondrous way, he returned to prominence when a cineaste found him working in a toy shop years after World War I. Today, his greatest surviving film, *A Trip to the Moon*, remains one of the most treasured of silent movies. In fact, in 2012 the electronic-music duo Air created a soundtrack album to coincide with the film's recent restoration.

ABOVE & RIGHT: After going bankrupt and losing his beloved theater in the 1920s, Georges Méliès really did work in a toy shop at the Gare Montparnasse. At right, the real Méliès, who is played by Ben Kingsley in the film (above).

V. FILM PRESERVATION

Though never explicitly expressed, *Hugo* touches on one of Scorsese's greatest causes: film preservation. Scorsese has been a vocal advocate for restoring older film negatives since the 1980s, and in subsequent years he has been behind two important preservation organizations, the Film Foundation and the World Cinema Foundation.

After the release of *Hugo*, Scorsese told *Variety*, "We need to remember that the loss of over 75 percent of silent cinema to deterioration isn't just a matter of rhetoric or propaganda—that's for real. We need to remember that films are being lost all the time, and that we only find out that they're lost after the fact: they don't explode, they just quietly deteriorate. We need to remember … that the work is constant and not at all glamorous. For every success story like the discovery and restoration of the John Ford silent picture *Upstream*, there are thousands of other pictures that need to be located, or properly restored, or preserved, or all of the above. In short, we need to remember, period. And we need to act, without waiting for someone else to do it."

In *Hugo*, this concern arises when Méliès scholar René Tabard (Michael Stuhlbarg) shows Méliès' wife Mama Jeanne (Helen McCrory) one of her husband's films—which shocks her, since she believed that his hundreds of movies were lost. When he sees his seminal sci-fi work *A Trip to the Moon* (*Le Voyage dans la Lune*) for the first time since the war, Méliès is astonished, explaining through an elaborate flashback how he became a filmmaker, the joy he once had making movies with his wife, and his reasons for later selling all his films to a company that melted them down into chemicals for women's shoes. Part of *Hugo*'s happy ending is Méliès receiving his belated due as a great artist in front of a large, ecstatic audience—but perhaps just as important is Tabard's announcement to the crowd that an extensive search has rounded up more than 80 Méliès films, although that's only a small percentage of the more than 500 he made before World War I.

In a 2013 speech at the Kennedy Center in Washington, DC, Scorsese declared, "Since [the 1980s], I think there actually has been a shift in consciousness and much more awareness of the need for preservation, which is ongoing… We're face to face with images all the time in a way that we never have been before. And that's why I believe we need to stress visual literacy in our schools. Young people need to understand that not all images are there to be consumed like fast food and then forgotten—we need to educate them to understand the difference between moving images that engage their humanity and their intelligence, and moving images that are just selling them something."

An artist like Méliès, part of the silent era when film preservation wasn't taken so seriously, risks being forgotten. Scorsese's organizations seek to keep that from happening, but perhaps a popular mainstream movie such as *Hugo* makes the point more potently.

BELOW: A still from Méliès' original *A Trip to the Moon*.

OPPOSITE (TOP TWO): Méliès' glass studio in Montreuil, France.

OPPOSITE (BOTTOM TWO): Images from Méliès' fantastical films, *A Trip to the Moon* and *Kingdom of the Fairies*.

SUMMARY OF TECHNIQUE

1. PAYING HOMAGE

Hugo's visual design replicates the look of the movies made by one of its central characters, Georges Méliès. Additionally, Scorsese drew inspiration from the Lumière brothers, who first excited Méliès about cinema's potential. But rather than making a soulless homage, *Hugo* is energized by these creative choices, producing a movie that feels of its period, while incorporating digital and 3D.

2. TECHNOLOGY AS A HELPFUL TOOL

When Scorsese made *Hugo*, 3D was experiencing a renaissance thanks to James Cameron's *Avatar*. Scorsese's use of the technology transcends gimmick. As his collaborators said, 3D forced them to rethink their approach to making movies, pushing them into new terrain.

3. ADAPTATION

Working from *The Invention of Hugo Cabret*, Scorsese and screenwriter John Logan sought to capture the spirit of Brian Selznick's novel while translating it to film. Even production designer Dante Ferretti brought a copy of the book onto the set to help remind himself of the initial vision for the project. *Hugo* is an illustration of what happens when a filmmaker understands what made the source material special and manages to preserve that vision for the big screen.

4. JOY

Because of the darkness lurking at the heart of many Scorsese movies, it's easy to forget what passion the filmmaker brings to his projects. But with *Hugo*, that joy is far more palpable—in part, because the movie was inspired by his daughter, and in part because the movie's themes speak directly to what matters most to him. A film that appeals to our core beliefs and interests will almost always produce superior work.

SELECTED BIBLIOGRAPHY

MEAN STREETS

Angard, Susan, "Kent Wakeford: Redefining American Cinematography in *Mean Streets*," www.huffingtonpost.com, March 5, 2009

Hill, Logan, "Spike Lee, Still Gliding to Success," www.nytimes.com, November 20, 2013

Kenny, Glenn, "Doing the Right Thing," www.dga.org, Spring 2008

Morgan, David, "Interview With Actor Harvey Keitel," www.wideanglecloseup.com, 1992

Schickel, Richard, *Conversations With Scorsese* (New York: Alfred A. Knopf, 2011)

Scorsese, Martin, Martin Scorsese: Interviews, ed. Peter Brunette (Jackson: University Press of Mississippi, 1999)

TAXI DRIVER

Balfour, Brad, "Martin Scorsese and Paul Schrader," www.popentertainment.com, March 15, 2012

Bliss, Michael and Nigel, *Doing It Right: The Best Criticism on Sam Peckinpah's* The Wild Bunch, ed. Michael Bliss (Carbondale and Edwardsville: Southern Illinois University Press, 1994)

DeCurtis, Anthony, *In Other Words: Artists Talk about Life and Work,* Hal Leonard, 2005, Milwaukee

Ebert, Roger, "Interview With Martin Scorsese," www.rogerebert.com, March 7, 1976

Ebert, Roger, "Scorsese Learns From Those Who Before Him," www.rogerebert.com, January 11, 1998

Ettedgui, Peter, Screencraft: Cinematography (Woburn: Focal Press, 1998)

Kelly, Mary Pat, *Martin Scorsese: A Journey* (New York: Thunder's Mouth Press, 2004)

Schaefer, Dennis and Salvato, Larry, *Masters of Light: Conversations With Contemporary Cinematographers* (Berkley and Los Angeles: University of California Press, 2013)

Simon, Alex, "Cybill Shepherd: The Comeback Kid," www.thehollywoodinterview.blogspot.com, Janary 23, 2008

THE LAST WALTZ

Baer, Joshua, "The Robbie Robertson Interview," *Musician,* May 1982

Biskind, Peter, *Easy Riders, Raging Bulls: How the Sex 'n' Drugs 'n' Rock 'n' Roll Generation Saved Hollywood,* Simon & Schuster, 1998, New York, 376

DeRiso, Nick, "Something Else! Interview: John Simon on the Band, fixing The Last Waltz, and taking credit," www.somethingelsereviews.com, January 29, 2014

Helm, Levon, "Do it, puke, and get out," www.independent.co.uk, April 10, 1994

"Levon Helm: The 2007 Fresh Air Interview" (audio), www.npr.org, April 19, 2012

Helm, Levon with Davis, Stephen, *This Wheel's on Fire: Levon Helm and the Story of The Band* (Chicago: A Cappella Books, 2013)

Hodenfield, Chris, "*The Last Waltz*: A Concert Becomes a Legend," www.rollingstone.com, June 1, 1978

Hoskyns, Barney, *Across the Great Divide: The Band and America* (Milwaukee: Hal Leonard, 2006)

Minturn, Neil, *The Last Waltz of The Band* (Missoula: The College Music Society, 2005)

Schickel, Richard, *Conversations With Scorsese*

Scorsese, Martin, *Martin Scorsese: Interviews,* ed. Peter Brunette

Scorsese, Martin, *Scorsese on Scorsese: Revised Edition,* eds. Ian Christie and David Thompson (London: Faber & Faber, 2003)

RAGING BULL

Boyle, Robert F., "Boris Leven: Setting the Scene for Movie World," www.latimes.com, November 9, 1986

Bunce, Steve, "Sugar Ray Robinson and Jake LaMotta created the perfect ring rivalry," www.independent.co.uk, November 17, 2014

Dougan, Andy, *Untouchable: A Biography of Robert De Niro* (New York: Thunder's Mouth Press, 2002)

Kilgannon, Corey, "Fighting a Bull, and the Fear of Obscurity," www.nytimes.com, February 7, 2005

Rausch, Andrew J., The Films of Martin Scorsese and Robert De Niro (Lanham, Maryland: Scarecrow Press, 2010)

Schaefer Dennis and Salvato, Larry *Masters of Light: Conversations With Contemporary Cinematographers*

Schickel, Richard, "Brutal Attraction: The Making of *Raging Bull*," www.vanityfair.com, March 2010

Tapley, Kristopher, "Martin Scorsese talks *Mean Streets, Taxi Driver* and rediscovering that childlike spark with *Hugo,*" www.hitfix.com, January 31, 2012

THE KING OF COMEDY

Altobello, Stephen (dir.), *A Shot at the Top: The Making of* The King of Comedy, Automat Pictures, 2002

Macaulay, Scott, "Scorsese, De Niro, Lewis and Bernhard Recall *The King of Comedy,*" www.filmmakermagazine.com, May 1, 2013

Rausch, Andrew J., *The Films of Martin Scorsese and Robert De Niro*

Schickel, Richard, *Conversations With Scorsese*

Scorsese, Martin, *Scorsese on Scorsese: Revised Edition,* eds. Ian Christie and David Thompson

Toro, Gabe, "Tribeca: Robert De Niro, Martin Scorsese & Jerry Lewis Reflect On *The King Of Comedy*, Improv, Deleted Scenes & More," http://blogs.indiewire.com/theplaylist/, April 29, 2013

Zuckoff, Mitchell, *Robert Altman: The Oral Biography* (New York: Alfred A. Knopf, 2009)

GOODFELLAS

Ballhaus, Michael, *Michael Ballhaus* (Bydgoszcz: Plus Camerimage, 2010)

"Ex-Wiseguy Henry Hill Always Had 'A Ringside Table,'" (audio interview) www.npr.org, June 15, 2012

Finke, Nikki, "Not Your Typical Wise Guy," www.latimes.com, September 16, 1990

Getting Made: The Making of Goodfellas (documentary film, written by Jonah Kaplan), Automat Pictures, 2004

"Getting Made the Scorsese Way," www.gq.com, October 2010

"Paul Thomas Anderson's Ten Films That Influenced *Boogie Nights*" *Neon Magazine*, August 1998

Pileggi, Nicholas, *Wiseguy: The 25th Anniversary Edition* (New York: Simon & Schuster)

Scorsese, Martin, *Scorsese on Scorsese: Revised Edition*, eds. Ian Christie and David Thompson

Seifried, Ron, "The Steady Approach: An Interview With Steadicam Inventor Garrett Brown," www.bhphotovideo.com, 2013

THE AGE OF INNOCENCE

Ebert, Roger, *Scorsese by Ebert* (Chicago: The University of Chicago Press, 2008)

Schickel, Richard, *Conversations With Scorsese*

Scorsese, Martin, *Scorsese on Scorsese: Revised Edition*, eds. Ian Christie and David Thompson

Stanley Kubrick: A Life in Pictures (documentary film directed by Jan Harlan), Warner Bros., 2001

GANGS OF NEW YORK

Armstrong, Vic, *The True Adventures of the World's Greatest Stuntman: My Life as Indiana Jones, James Bond, Superman and Other Movie Heroes* (London: Titan, 2011)

Ballhaus, Michael, *Michael Ballhaus*

Bibbiani, William, "Vic Armstrong on Being The World's Greatest Stuntman," www.craveonline.com, May 16, 2011

Bosley, Rachael K., "Native Sons," www.theasc.com, January 2003

Buchanan, Kyle, "Toronto: Harvey Weinstein Remembers the DiCaprio-vs.-Day-Lewis Rivalry on *Gangs of New York*," www.vulture.com, September 12, 2013

Gangs of New York (DVD director's audio commentary), Miramax, 2003

Giroux, Jack, "25 Things We Learned From Martin Scorsese's *Gangs of New York Commentary*," www.filmschoolrejects.com, December 19, 2013

Halligan, Fionnuala, *FilmCraft: Production Design* (Lewes: Ilex, 2012)

Kavner, Lucas, "Vic Armstrong, World's Greatest Stuntman, Looks Back," www.huffingtonpost.com, May 10, 2011

Schickel, Richard, *Conversations With Scorsese*

THE DEPARTED

Ballhaus, Michael, *Michael Ballhaus*

Hiscock, John, "The day Mad Jack drew a gun on set," www.telegraph.co.uk, September 22, 2006

Murray, Rebecca, "Leonardo DiCaprio Talks About The Departed," http://movies.about.com, 2008

Pilkington, Ed, "A history of violence," www.theguardian.com, October 6, 2006

Pinkerton, Nick, "Interview: Thelma Schoonmaker," www.filmcomment.com, March 31, 2014

Pizzello, Stephen, "Deep Cover," www.theasc.com, October 2006

Schickel, Richard, *Conversations With Scorsese*

Tapley, Kristopher, "Thelma Schoonmaker Recalls an Unpredictable Jack Nicholson in Best Picture Winner *The Departed*," www.hitfix.com, December 22, 2013

HUGO

Bowe, John, "Martin Scorsese's Magical *Hugo*," www.nytimes.com, November 2, 2011

Grosz, Christy, "Scorsese talks preservation," www.variety.com, January 1, 2012

Halligan, Fionnuala, *FilmCraft: Production Design*

Hardie, Giles, "Martin Scorsese interview," www.smh.com.au, June 24, 2012

Hyman, Vicki, "*Hugo Cabret* creator Brian Selznick says Martin Scorsese movie may be better than his beloved book," www.nj.com, November 20, 2011

Logan, John (screenplay by), *Hugo: The Shooting Script* (New York: Newmarket Press, 2011)

"Martin Scorsese Lecture" (tran), www.neh.gov, March/April, 2013

"Secrets Unlocked," www.britishcinematographer.co.uk

Vulliamy, Ed, "Brian Selznick: how Scorsese's *Hugo* drew inspiration from his magical book," www.theguardian.com, February 11, 2012

INDEX

PICTURE CREDITS

Alamy A F Archive 13, 21, 31 above left & right, 32 above & below left, 33 below, 34 left, 42 left & below right, 43 left & right, 45 below, 47 left, 48 below, 55 above & below, 56, 57 below, 61 above & below, 69 below, 74, 75, 80 below, 85 below left, 88 below, 92–3, 95 above right & below, 96 below left & right, 97 above & below left, 101 above & below, 104–5, 106, 107, 108, 111 above, 113, 114–15, 116–17, 118, 120, 121 above & below, 122, 123 above left, right & below right, 124 above & below right, 125 above below, 126 below, 133 above & below, 134, 134–5, 135 below, 137 left; Cineclassico 37 below; Dan Callister 81 above; Everett Collection Historical 57 above; Globe Photos/Zuma Press 48 above, 49 above, 100 left; Granamour Weems Collection 19 below; Interfoto 36 below right, 136 center; MARKA 100–101; Moviestore Collection Ltd   10–11, 15 above, 16, 23 below, 24, 26–7, 29 below, 30 left & right, 33 above & center, 36 above left & above right, 42 above right, 53, 60, 62, 62–3, 64–5, 72, 76–7, 78–9, 81 below, 85 right, 88 above, 94, 96 above left, 111 below, 119 above, 128–9, 135 above, 138; Photos12 14, 15 below, 18, 19 above, 20 above left & right, 22–3, 31 below, 32 right, 44 left, 54 above, 67, 68, 69 above, 80 above, 85 above, 88–9, 89, 95 above left & center, 96 above right, 97 above right, 103, 112, 119 below, 123 below left, 126 above, 127, 130, 131, 132, 135 center, 136 above & below, 139 all; Pictorial Press 20 below, 34–5, 37 above, 52, 97 below right; The Art Archive 110 below

Courtesy **Garrett Brown** 83

Getty Images Elliott Landy 40–41, 44–5; Jeff Goode/Toronto Star 114 left; Michael Ochs Archive 46; Richard Blanshard 102; Richard E Aaron/Redferns 47 right

Courtesy **Martin Scorsese Collection** 58, 17, with permission from Paul Schrader, Schrader Productions 28–9 above

Press Association Images AP 38, 45 above, 54 below, Sean Dempsey/PA Archive 124 below left

The Academy of Motion Picture Arts and Sciences © Universal 59 below

The Kobal Collection 137 right; Edison 73; International Films Espanola/Alpine Productions 109 all; Phillip Caruso/Columbia 90–91, United Artists 50–51

ADDITIONAL CREDITS:

110 above is reproduced with the permission of the artist.

© 20th Century Fox 70–71, © Artisan Pictures 23 center, © Columbia 35, 98–9, © Harvest/Truth & Soul 22 above, © Warner Brothers 82–3, 84, 86–7

SPECIAL THANKS TO:

Marianne Bower of Martin Scorsese's office, for her generous assistance sourcing archive materials in the midst of shooting *Silence* in Taipei.